G000114581

# Tiling

## Julian Cassell
## Peter Parham

MARSHALL PUBLISHING · LONDON

**A Marshall Edition**
Conceived, edited and designed by
Marshall Editions
The Orangery
161 New Bond Street
London W1Y 9PA

First published in the UK in 2000
by Marshall Publishing Ltd
Copyright © 2000 Marshall Editions Ltd,
London UK

ISBN: 1-84028-368-8
Originated in Singapore by Chroma Graphics.
Printed and bound in China by Excel Printing.

**Project Editor** Felicity Jackson

**Designed by** Martin Lovelock
                  & John Round

**Photographer** Tim Ridley

**Illustrations** Chris Forsey

**Project Manager** Nicholas Barnard

**Managing Art Editor** Patrick Carpenter

**Managing Editor** Antonia Cunningham

**Editorial Director** Ellen Dupont

**Art Director** Dave Goodman

**Editorial Coordinator** Ros Highstead

**Production** Anna Pauletti

**Indexer** Hilary Bird

Front cover photography: **John Freeman** (top and
centre) **Robert Harding Picture Library** (bottom
left) **Tim Ridley** (bottom centre) **Dennis Gilbert/
View** (bottom right) Back cover: **Tim Ridley**

## Note

Every effort has been taken to ensure that all
information in this book is correct and compatible with
national standards generally accepted at the time of
publication. This book is not intended to replace
manufacturer's instructions in the use of their tools or
materials – always follow their safety guidelines. The
author and publisher disclaim any liability, loss, injury or
damage incurred as a consequence, directly or indirectly,
of the use and application of the contents of this book.

*The authors would like
to thank the following
companies for their
assistance in producing
this book:*

Bliss
Paradise Works
Arden Forest Estate
Alcester
Warwickshire
B49 6EH
Tel. 0870 0110800

Fired Earth
South Street
Sherborne
Dorset
DT9 3TD
Tel. 01935 817900

S M Flooring
65 Cheap Street
Sherborne
Dorset
DT9 3BA
Tel. 01935 815575

Dulux Decorator Centres
Altrincham
Cheshire
WA14 5PG
Tel. 0161 9683000

The DEVA Tap
Company
Brooklands Mill
English Street
Leigh
Lancashire
WN7 3EH
Tel. 01942 680177

Dave Marsh Hardware
Fore Street
Castle Cary
Somerset
BA7 7BG
Tel. 01963 350316

The English Stamp
Company
Worth Matravers
Dorset
BH19 3JP
Tel. 01929 439117

The Stencil Store
89 Lower Sloane Street
London
SW1 W8DA
Tel. 0171 823 6700

Tile Wise Ltd
12-14 Enterprise Mews
Sea King Road
Lynx Trading Estate
Yeovil
Somerset
BA20 2NZ
Tel. 01935 412220

Sharpe & Fisher (BS) Ltd
Mill Street
Wincanton
Somerset
BA9 9AP
Tel. 01963 33881

The Tile Market
Bardell Court
Houndstone Business Park
Yeovil
Somerset
BA20 2NZ
Tel. 01935 433331

Hewden Plant Hire
Station Road
Bruton
Somerset
BA10 0EH
Tel. 01749 812267

MGR Exports
Station Road
Bruton
Somerset
BA10 0EH
Tel. 01749 812460

*Further thanks goes to the
following individuals who
supplied props and general
assistance:*

Adele Parham, Emma
Isaacs, Katriena Veal, John
and Margaret Dearden,
Jakki Dearden, Rob
Mahoney, and Julia
Barnard.

# CONTENTS

# INTRODUCTION

Tiles have been used to provide decorative and hard-wearing surfaces for walls and floors for hundreds of years. Their influence continues to grow due to the ever-increasing choice and easy availability for the home decorator. In years gone by, tiling was considered the domain of the professional, and most homeowners would not have dreamt of attempting to tile a basin splashback, let alone an entire room. Nowadays, all major DIY outlets have a tiling department, and modern products and tools are much easier to use. Tiling is now a job in the home that anyone can tackle and achieve a good result. This book guides you through all the necessary techniques for any tiling project, showing you how to solve problems along the way and produce a professional result that will enhance your home for the enjoyment of your family and the admiration of your friends.

## TILING SUCCESSFULLY

Taking it slowly is the secret of good tiling. When a project fails to live up to expectations, it can generally be put down to rushing, rather than any glaring errors in technique. It takes more time to grasp the methodology of tiling than that of other home DIY tasks that can be done quickly, with an instant result. To build up confidence with tiling materials and tools, you have to be patient and work slowly – it is far better to take longer with the preparation and execution than regret a poor finish for many years to come. Enjoy the process of tiling – don't look on it as a chore. Aim to improve your technique and, above all, be creative with patterns and designs, because it gives great personal satisfaction when all your effort produces a truly individual look. By all means look through magazines for ideas, but adding your own personal touch is always the most pleasing part of any home decorating project – and tiling is no exception.

## BEING PREPARED

Preparation is a vital part of any home decorating project and can make the difference between an average finish and one that you can be proud of. Although preparation is always the least attractive of any decorating task, it must be carried out thoroughly to ensure good results. Chapter 1 takes you through the entire process of planning and preparing, from choosing tiles to the preparation of surfaces for tile application. There is plenty of advice on how to treat different surfaces and what techniques will produce the best results.

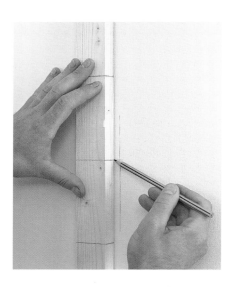

## ESTABLISHING A SOUND TECHNIQUE

A good tiling technique is built on a sound understanding of basic rules and methods. Establishing good habits from the start with the straightforward aspects of tiling will stand you in good stead when you come to tackle the more demanding tasks. Chapter 2 explains the basic tiling technique, from laying first tiles through to developing a sound method for simple tile cutting.

## DEALING WITH AWKWARD AREAS

Awkward areas are really defined by the fact that they require more planning or, in most cases, intricate tile cutting. They are, in fact, really just a further development of the basic tiling technique. Chapter 3 guides you through a variety of awkward situations that you might come across, providing the solutions and demonstrating that keeping to a system makes it possible to overcome any obstacle when tiling.

## ADVENTUROUS TILING

Expressing your individual preference is a vital part of enjoying tiling, and Chapter 4 shows you how to stray away from the more traditional looks and create your own unique designs. The basics remain the same but some additional techniques for combining tile sizes and producing different patterns are outlined in this chapter, adding to the fundamental skills learnt earlier in the book.

## TILING FLOORS

Many of the techniques used on a vertical wall surface can be transferred to floor tiling, as the general appearance of the tiles remains the same. However, because of their function, floor tiles need to be more hard-wearing, and this means that the methods of preparation and application do vary slightly. These subtle changes in approach are explained in detail in Chapter 5, enabling you to extend your tiling repertoire to the household floors as well as walls.

## MAINTAINING SURFACES

As with all decorated surfaces, it is important to know the best methods of mainting them and how to carry out minor repairs. By design, tiles are extremely hard-wearing and have an appreciable lifespan, whether on the walls or on the floor. Chapter 6 demonstrates how to keep tiles looking as good as possible and gives advice on how to lengthen their lifespan with little effort.

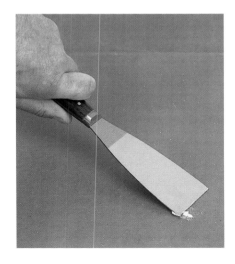

# PROGRESSIVE TILING

This book caters for both the novice and the more experienced tiler, teaching the beginner all the basic techniques whilst enabling the more skilful to fill in any gaps in their knowledge before progressing to new and exciting challenges. Much of the fundamental knowledge and understanding found in any form of decorating is carried over into the tiling field, and this helps the process of forming ideas, solving problems and adapting to different situations. After all, the decorator is concerned with improving the look of a room, and applying tiles is no different in this respect from applying paint or paper. The concise and accurate instructions given in the following chapters, linked with the variety of ideas and choices they provide, make this book an invaluable tool for helping you create the perfect tiled finish, and enable you to integrate tiled surfaces into the rest of the decoration in your home.

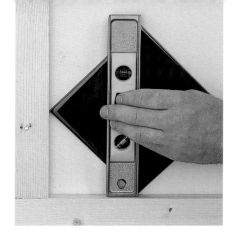

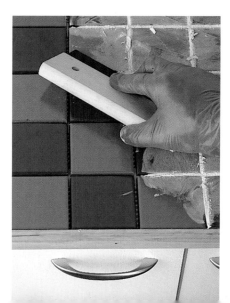

# Planning and Preparation

# PLANNING AND PREPARATION

*Careful planning of a tiling project is the key to producing a good overall finish. Although choosing patterns, designs and colours are all important, as is the actual tiling technique, making sure that surfaces are prepared and a logical progression is carried out are the vital ingredients of any tiling project. Tiles are expensive, and starting off with the wrong strategy can prove costly. The whole tiling experience should be thought out and done slowly, not rushed. Once they are applied, tiles are relatively permanent, and, unlike changing one coat of paint for another, major work is required to change their appearance. It is therefore worth taking a little extra time to make important choices and to follow the correct procedures that ensure a finish you will be proud of.*

# TOOLS AND EQUIPMENT

**H**aving the correct tools and equipment is an essential part of any tiling project. In addition to the general-purpose tools found in a standard household toolbox, there are a number of items, designed specifically for tiling, that you will need. It is always better to buy quality tools – these will last longer than cheaper versions, and will be more accurate and easier to use.

## PREPARATION

Protective gloves          Scraper     Tape measure     Hammer

Grout raker

Abrasive paper

Pencil

Felt-tip pen

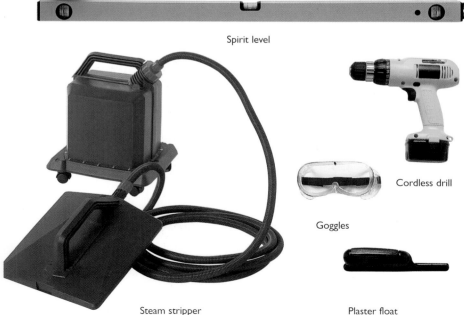

Spirit level

Steam stripper

Goggles

Cordless drill

Plaster float

# CUTTING

Score-and snap-tool

Tile cutter

Nibblers

Tile saw

Tile-cutting machine

Workbench

Cold chisel

Tile file

# TILING

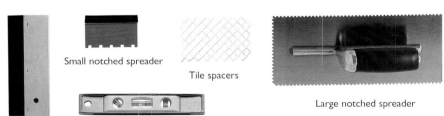

Small notched spreader

Tile spacers

Large notched spreader

Grout spreader    Torpedo level

# FINISHING

Grout shaper

Trowel    Cotton rag    Sponge

Sealant
dispenser

# PLANNING A SCHEME

P lanning a scheme of tiling is an area that combines personal preference with practicalities. Although most tiles can be applied anywhere in the home, you need to consider how the tiles will fit into a particular scheme in a room and how practical they will be.

**Covering surfaces:** tiles are very decorative and they can be used to cover any of the wall surfaces in a room. A tiled wall surface can be very impressive, whether the tiles are highly patterned or a plain design. A tiling project of this size requires plenty of time to plan it properly and a certain amount of skill when it comes to tile application and starting in the correct place on the surface to be tiled.

**Creating a dado:** tiling up to dado level allows the tiles to have an equal standing with the rest of the room's decoration. Combining paper and paint with tiles requires a certain amount of imagination to coordinate the whole scheme, and it puts a greater emphasis on matching texture and finish in order to get the desired effect.

Covering the floor: floor tiles combine the highly practical function of being the most hard-wearing of floorings with huge decorative appeal. It is vital to keep tiles aligned and level for a good effect; careful preparation and accurate tile application are essential if you want to create a desirable floor tile finish.

Smaller areas: the simple tiling of a splashback can effect the whole feel of a room. The splashback's colour, size and pattern all combine to give the room a finished look. Because smaller areas of tiles tend to come in for more scrutiny, the neatness and accuracy of the tiling is vital.

## PLANNING IDEAS

- Colour: whether complementing other decorations, or forming the main theme, always obtain samples from your supplier before making a final choice, then the tiles can be compared and tried in the actual room that is being decorated. Make sure you compare paint colour swatches with tiles, as well as carpet and wallpaper samples, if necessary.
- Size: there are no hard and fast rules on the best size of tiles for a particular room, but it is worth remembering that large tiles are more awkward when it comes to making fiddly cuts, and smaller tiles take longer to apply.

- Pattern: often a few patterned tiles within a decorating scheme produce the best results – too many highly patterned tiles can be overwhelming, especially in a small room, and may spoil the overall look.
- Expense: almost without exception, the more expensive the tiles, the more attractive and better quality they will be. However, combining more expensive tiles with cheaper alternatives can often work very well in a scheme. It is also worth considering how long you are likely to stay in the house, and whether the extra expense will be beneficial in the long term.

# TYPES OF TILE

There is a vast range of tiles to choose from, which means that in most cases it is possible to find exactly the size, finish and colour required. Most suppliers have sample boards to show more extensive examples of finished surfaces, and some produce catalogues of tiled interiors to help you choose. It is always a good idea to use whatever aids are available to help you pick the finish you want.

## STANDARD TILES

This group of tiles includes the more traditional-looking tiles, with a wide range of relatively simple colour themes and design.

Hand-made painted tile

Picture tile

Relief picture tile

Rectangular wall tile

Glazed terracotta tile

Unglazed terracotta tile

## BORDER TILES

The choice of border tiles is constantly increasing, with different sizes, types of pattern and variety of textures, all adding to the large range already available.

Relief border tile

Standard border tile

Dado border tile

Mitred quadrant tile

Relief tile slips

## ALTERNATIVE TILES

Non-standard tiles are becoming increasingly popular, with sizes varying from small mosaics to larger wall tiles, making all manner of different effects and finishes possible.

Octagonal tile

Marble tile

Sheet mosaic  Tiled scene   Inset tiles

Marble floor tile

## FLOOR TILES

Floor tiles are thicker and more hard-wearing than wall tiles. The range of tiles is slightly more limited, but the manufacturers are constantly coming up with new ideas for finishes.

Quarry tile  Mosaic floor tile

Standard floor tile  Slate floor tile

# ORDER OF WORK

I t is always difficult to decide where to start on a particular wall, as most of them are not perfectly square and free of obstacles. Instructions for dealing with particular situations are dealt with in other chapters. However, it is worth taking time at the planning stage to consider any particular obstacles that will have to be taken into account, what the most common problem areas are likely to be, and how you can best overcome them.

## BATHROOMS

The bathroom is the one room in the house that is usually totally or partially tiled, and it will undoubtably contain areas that need some considerable planning before you can begin to tile. A simple bath scenario is outlined below and gives some valuable pointers on the most suitable order of work.

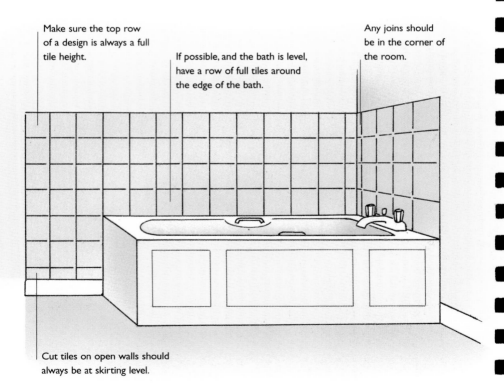

Make sure the top row of a design is always a full tile height.

If possible, and the bath is level, have a row of full tiles around the edge of the bath.

Any joins should be in the corner of the room.

Cut tiles on open walls should always be at skirting level.

# KITCHENS

Kitchens provide many obstacles similar to those found in bathrooms, with additional problem areas such as power points. This example also shows the need for careful planning around windows.

Tiles should always reach up to the underside of wall units.

Cuts in window tiles should be around the frame, rather than at the front of the sill.

Any joins should be in the corner of the room.

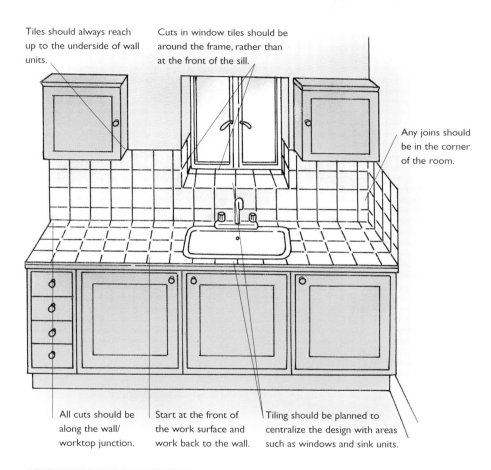

All cuts should be along the wall/ worktop junction.

Start at the front of the work surface and work back to the wall.

Tiling should be planned to centralize the design with areas such as windows and sink units.

## ESTIMATING QUANTITIES

There is no secret to estimating the quantity of tiles required for a job – it is all a matter of simple mathematics. Measure the dimensions of the area to be tiled in order to attain the surface area. Divide the surface area of one tile into this figure and this will give you the number of tiles required. It is always worth adding on 10 percent extra to account for cutting and breakages. To make measuring easier, it is worth breaking down complicated surfaces into smaller areas, so the calculations are more accurate.

# PREPARING WALLS

C reating a sound surface on which to tile is essential. Not only will this produce better results when new tiles are applied, it will also make the actual tiling process much easier. A new wall surface is the ideal starting point for tiling, but it is often the case that an old tiled surface is being replaced.

## EXISTING TILES

A previously tiled surface can be tiled over if it is sound and level. If the old tiles are firmly stuck to the wall, new tiles may be applied directly over the top of them. Some minor repairs may be necessary to ensure that the surface is totally sound. Remove any loose old tiles before beginning the preparation.

**Filling space:** fill the space left by the removal of old tiles with an all purpose decorating filler. Before applying the filler, dust out the hole thoroughly to ensure good adhesion. Build up the filler level until it is flush with the surrounding tiles.

**Using old tiles:** an alternative to using filler in the space left by loose old tiles is to use old tiles of the same size as those on the wall. Simply apply some adhesive to the tile, and use it to fill the hole. Again, make sure that the tile surface is flush with the surrounding area of tiles.

**Sanding tiles:** after the old tiled surface has been filled, wash it down with soapy water, then rinse well. Sand the entire tiled area with silicone carbide paper. This will scratch the glaze and help provide a key for the adhesive. Make sure you sand every single tile to get the best possible adhesion of new tile to old.

## WALL REPAIR

When an old tiled surface is badly damaged or loose, it cannot be used as the base for retiling and must be totally stripped away. Although this is a longer process than simple repairs on existing tile surfaces, you will reap the benefit when the new tiles are applied.

Removing old tiles: old tiles are best removed using a hammer and cold chisel. Try not to dig into the wall with the chisel, as this will damage the surface of the wall. Position the chisel point exactly on the junction between tile and wall before hitting it with the hammer. Wear protective goggles to protect your eyes from flying tile splinters and debris.

Removing old tile adhesive: once tiles are removed, there is often a large amount of residual old tile adhesive left on the wall. A steam stripper is ideal for softening the hard adhesive before removing it with a scraper. Steam strippers vary, so be sure to read the operating and safety instructions before use.

Patch plastering: where walls are particularly rough, it may be necessary to skim some areas with a coat of all-purpose plaster to make the surface level enough for tiling. Seal the wall area with a PVA solution (five parts water to one part PVA) before applying the plaster.

### PREPARATION ESSENTIALS

- Never tile over wallpaper as the weight of the tiles will gradually pull the paper away from the wall surface. Wallpaper must be stripped before tiling.
- Gloss surfaces must be sanded before tiling over them, to provide a key for the new tiles.
- Old and new plaster surfaces must be sealed with a PVA solution (five parts water to one part PVA) before tiling them.

# CREATING A FRESH SURFACE

I n many situations, such as working around baths or tiling up to dado level, it is easier to create a totally flat fresh surface on which to tile. The simplest way of producing a new surface is to use a flat building board such as MDF, which is economical and easy to work with. Always wear a dust mask when sawing MDF to prevent inhalation of dust particles.

## FLUSH PANELLING

MDF is useful when gaps around the bath make tiling difficult. It makes a nice neat junction between the bath and the finished tile surface. MDF board can be applied directly to the wall surface to create a very smooth flush base on which to tile. Board thickness should be around 9 mm ($\frac{3}{8}$ in).

1 Cut the sheet of MDF to the required size and position it on the edge of the bath. To create a totally waterproof seal, apply some silicone sealant to the MDF/bath junction.

2 Once positioned, drill pilot holes through the sheet using a wood drill bit, and switch to a masonry bit once you hit the wall. Or, if you are using concrete anchor screws, an all-purpose drill bit will be supplied with the screws. Increase the entrance size (see below).

3 If using standard screws, insert a wall plug into the hole before inserting the screw. Concrete anchor screws (shown here) can be inserted directly into the wall. Insert screws every 30 cm (12 in), in both horizontal and vertical directions, until the sheet is fixed.

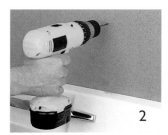

### INCREASING THE HOLE SIZE

Use a countersink bit to increase the entrance size of the drilled hole. This will allow the screw head to sit flush with the MDF surface once it is screwed in.

# PANELLING ON A FRAME

Where wall surfaces are very uneven, you may need to fix MDF sheets to a frame on the wall. This will cover any large depressions in the wall surface and give an even surface for tiling. Use concrete anchor screws for this wood/masonry combination.

1 Fix 5 x 2.5 cm (2 x 1 in) battens vertically to the wall, up to the height that is to be tiled. Fix the battens 30 cm (12 in) apart, ensuring that they are vertical by checking with a long spirit level.

2 Pack uneven areas in the wall by hammering in wedges of wood behind battens that do not sit flush with the wall surface. This will ensure that the battens are vertical to the floor and also to the actual wall surface. Fix the wedges in place with a nail if they start to slip.

3 Place a cut sheet of MDF on the battened wall surface, then mark off vertical pencil lines on the MDF surface to show where it should be fixed. These vertical lines should correspond with the battens fixed to the wall. Nail along each line every 25 cm (10 in) to fix the MDF to the battens.

4 Nail a further length of batten to the top of the framework to give a neat fixed level to tile up to. The vertical pencil guidelines on the MDF surface will show where the fixing points are. A decorative dado rail can be used instead of the batten, or a moulding can be attached to the front of the batten when the tiling is finished.

# BOXING IN

**A**s well as wall surfaces, there are other areas that may require preparation before you can start tiling. Unsightly pipes, for example, can be boxed in and then the box can be tiled to create a decorative surface.

## SIMPLE BOXING

Boxing in requires a combination of wooden battens and building board to build a sturdy framework around the pipes. MDF of 18 mm (¾ in) thickness is ideal, with 5 x 2.5 cm (2 x 1 in) batten as support. Boxing is best screwed together to provide stronger joints and fixing points. To ensure a flush surface for tiling, countersink the drill holes (see page 20).

**1** Attach a batten to the wall directly above the pipes and fix a further batten to the floor. Make sure the floor batten runs parallel to the wall surface, and that it is positioned further away from the wall than the pipe. Use screws that do not go below the level of the floorboards otherwise you may damage pipes or cables below floor level or, even more importantly, you may injure yourself.

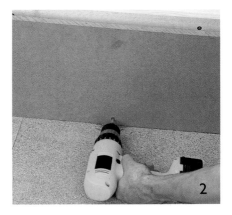

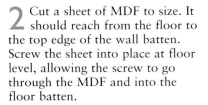

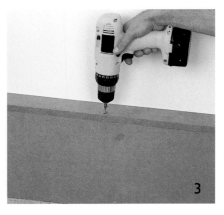

**2** Cut a sheet of MDF to size. It should reach from the floor to the top edge of the wall batten. Screw the sheet into place at floor level, allowing the screw to go through the MDF and into the floor batten.

**3** Cut a second piece of MDF the width of the wall to the front face of the fixed MDF. Fix it to the wall batten and fixed sheet of MDF with screws. Make sure that the corner join is precise. Continue until the pipes are totally boxed in.

## BOXING IN TIPS

Boxing in is not always completely straightforward and you may need to take the following considerations into account when covering up areas of wall. Although accuracy is important, remember that the boxing will be covered, so a perfect finish at this stage is not essential.

**Cutting curves:** use a jigsaw to cut curves in the board where you need to allow pipes to protrude through the boxing. Always follow the manufacturer's safety precautions when using a jigsaw and never place your hand in front of the blade of the saw or in the direction you are cutting the board.

**Leaving access:** many pipes have shut-off valves, stopcocks or inspection joints, depending on the particular function of the pipe. You need to make inspection hatches in the boxing to allow access to these points. Cutting in a small hatch and fitting it with magnetic catches is the ideal solution.

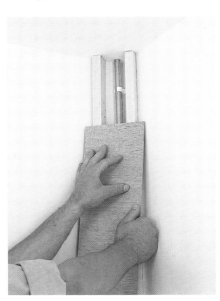

**Corner boxing:** corners may either be boxed in as shown on the opposite page, but vertically, or a single panel can be used to shut off the corner. This method requires making a mitred cut through a length of batten to provide a 45 degree angle for attachment of the batten to either side of the corner junction. A thinner building board such as ply can then be cut to fit across the corner. Attach the ply to the batten using panel pins or small screws.

# FINAL PLANNING

B efore starting to tile, prepare the working area and make sure that all the tools and equipment you need are to hand. There are a few final preparations that will make life much easier, speed up the tiling process, and lead to a better overall finish.

**Breaking up spacers:** tile spacers are usually manufactured in sheets and need to be broken into single units before they can be used. It saves a great deal of time if several sheets are broken up before tiling starts, then you can achieve an easy rhythm of applying a tile with one hand and fitting a spacer with the other.

**Shuffling tiles:** there can be slight colour differences between tile batches, and even within the same box shades sometimes vary slightly from one end of the box to the other. Mix or shuffle tiles from different boxes before starting so that any variations will be 'diluted' across the whole wall surface. Although this problem is most common with strongly coloured tiles, even white tiles should be shuffled to ensure an even finish.

## BE PREPARED

- Have a bucket of clean water and a cloth to hand so that surfaces can be kept clean at all times.
- A second bucket of clean water can be used for temporary storage of tools during breaks. This prevents adhesive on items like notched spreaders from going hard, which

will make further application to the wall more difficult.
- Protect basins, baths and any fixtures or fittings with dust sheets. Adhesive splashes can be difficult to remove from any surface once they have hardened, so it is best to prevent them in the first place.

# Tiling Techniques

# TILING TECHNIQUE

*Tiling requires a methodical approach with attention to detail. Once you have established a sound basic technique, you can tackle more difficult tiling projects. As with all decorating tasks, speed comes with practice: it is important to take your time rather than rushing to finish the job quickly. Even the most experienced tilers can always improve their technique, and professionals are always trying to achieve the perfect tiled surface. This chapter shows you how to tile walls, and demonstrates the few simple rules and procedures that are the basis for a sound tiling technique.*

# STARTING LEVEL

T iles have crisp, straight edges that give a very ordered and
precise finish when they are applied to the wall. Although this
is one of their attractive characteristics, it also means that poorly
applied or crooked tiles stand out, so it is important to start level
and tile from a secure, fixed base. Take time to determine the starting
point, as mistakes can be difficult to rectify once tiling has begun.

1 A tile gauge is essential for determining the best possible starting point on a wall surface. Cut a length of 5 x 2.5 cm (2 x 1 in) batten about 1.5 m (5 ft) long, or shorter if you are tiling a small area. Line up a row of tiles along the length of the batten with tile spacers between them. Using a pencil, mark off the position of each tile along one edge of the batten.

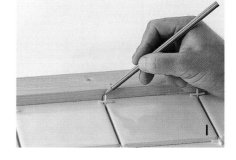

2 Find the central point of the wall or area to be tiled by measuring first vertically, and then horizontally, across the wall. Make sure the tape measure is level when measuring. Make a pencil mark at the centre. This acts as the point from which to centralize the entire design.

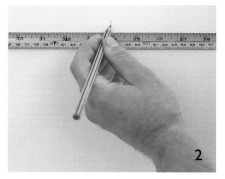

3 Use the tiling gauge to find how many rows of tiles you will need for the area you are going to tile. Hold the gauge vertically against the wall to show where the tile edges will fall once they are applied. Mark the positions off along the wall. Then hold the gauge horizontally and mark off again. It is unlikely that the tiles will fit exactly into the working area, so you will need to adjust the central point slightly so that any tiles you have to cut will be at the edges not in the centre (see pages 16-17).

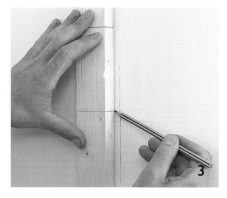

4 It is unlikely that the top of the
skirting board is exactly level, or
that the tile gauge has demonstrated
that the best position to start tiling is
directly on top of the skirting board.
The bottom level of tiles will
probably need to be cut. This means
that the starting point is where the
first row of full tiles will be applied,
and this is where a length of batten
should be fixed to provide a solid
base (see step 6). Ensure that the
batten is level.

5 Once the horizontal batten is
fixed, a vertical batten is required
to provide the starting point across
the other wall dimension. Fix the
batten where the first column of
vertical tiles will begin, using a level
to make sure that the batten is
completely vertical. Alternatively, the
vertical batten can be positioned at
the central point of the area to be
tiled, and tiling can progress towards
the corner, rather than away from it.
Either way is acceptable, as the sole
purpose of the vertical batten is to
maintain a rigid vertical line to butt
the tiles up against.

6 Attach the wall battens with
nails, but do not drive them all
the way into the wall. Leave a good
amount of the nail head showing, so
that the battens can be removed with
a claw hammer once the tiles have
been applied and the adhesive has
dried. Masonry nails tend to make
the best batten fixings, but on dry
lined or stud walls it may be easier
to use screws.

# APPLYING ADHESIVE

A dhesive must be applied evenly to ensure that the tiles will sit correctly on the wall surface. You can use ready-mixed adhesive, or powder that needs to be mixed with water. Both types are equally effective and there is no difference in technique when applying them.

## SMALL AREAS

**2**

In small, intricate tiling areas, it is easier if you use smaller tools. You can apply the adhesive to the wall or to the back of the tiles. Adhesive starts to harden once it is exposed to the air, so applying it to a small area at a time reduces the possibility of it drying before the tile has been applied to the wall.

**Applying adhesive to tiles:** use a small notched spreader to apply adhesive directly to the back of tiles, removing any excess. The jagged teeth of the spreader create peaks and troughs along the adhesive surface, which improves adhesion when the tile is applied to the wall.

**Getting in corners:** a small notched spreader is the ideal tool for getting adhesive into tight corners. This is especially useful when laying the first tiles, which will need to be tight against the supporting battens. Beginners will also find that a small notched spreader is easier to use and creates less mess than a large one.

### ADHESIVE IDEAS

- When taking a break, always keep the lid on the adhesive tub to stop it drying out.
- If tiling a large area, use adhesive which requires mixing, as it is usually cheaper than ready-mixed varieties.
- For very small areas of wall, use 'tile and grout' adhesive – as the name

suggests, this can be used as grout as well as adhesive. Although it tends to be expensive, it is very economical in small areas as it eliminates the need to buy both an adhesive and a grout, which are difficult to buy separately in the small quantities you would need for this sort of area.

## LARGE AREAS

On large, open expanses of wall, adhesive can be spread over greater areas of the wall surface and the tiles can be applied relatively quickly. Use a larger notched spreader as it covers a large wall space much more quickly than a small spreader.

1 Use the flat broad surface of the notched spreader to dig adhesive out of its tub or bucket, then use a pressing, sweeping motion to apply it to the wall. Do not try to apply too much at a time as the adhesive will simply fall away around the sides of the spreader and onto the floor.

2 Draw the serrated edge of the spreader across the surface of the adhesive, creating furrows in its surface. Apply enough pressure for the points along the spreader's edge to touch the wall surface, but not enough for them to gouge into it. This creates an even coat that is the ideal surface on which to twist the first tiles, producing a firm bond between wall and tiles.

3 Do not cover more than 1 sq m (1 sq yd) of the wall at a time as the tiles must be applied while the adhesive is still wet and workable. It is better for beginners to start by covering an area half this size and gradually build up to the larger area.

# APPLYING THE FIRST TILES

T he first tiles are the most important in any tile design as they provide the starting point and base for the whole tiled area. Poor application at this stage can affect the entire finish, so you need to take great care when positioning the first tiles.

**2**

1 Place the first tile tight into the corner made by the horizontal and vertical battens. Use a slight twisting motion when pressing the tile onto the adhesive surface to ensure good contact between the back of the tile and the adhesive.

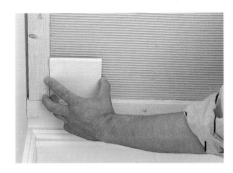

2 Continue to apply tiles in a row along the top of the horizontal batten. Apply spacers between every tile to ensure uniform gaps for grouting. Because of the batten, the spacers at the base of the first row of tiles have to be positioned pointing out from the tiled surface. These can be removed when the adhesive has dried, whereas other spacers on the wall surface are left in position to be grouted over.

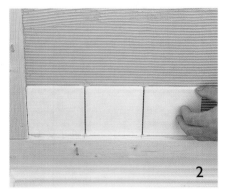

2

3 Check that the level is being maintained after every two rows of tiles. Use a torpedo level, held across three tiles at a time, to make sure that none of the tiles have slipped out of position. Take care not to get any adhesive on the torpedo level – clean it immediately if you do.

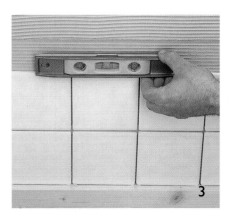

3

4 Once a large block of tiles is complete, hold a length of batten across the tiled surface, to check that they are all sitting flush. Any sunken or protruding tiles will be obvious and then any necessary adjustments can be made.

5 Adjustments to tile position must be carried out while the adhesive is still wet. Lever out sunken or protruding tiles with a scraper, taking care not to scratch or chip the tile surface.

6 For a sunken tile, apply more adhesive to the back of the tile with a small notched spreader. Reposition the tile on the wall, again using the wooden batten to check that it is now sitting flush with the surrounding tiled surface. For a protruding tile, simply remove some of the adhesive and reapply the tile to the wall.

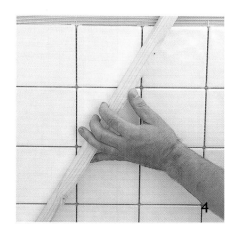

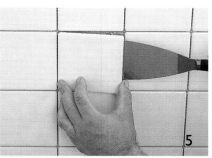

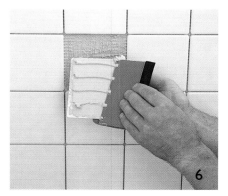

## WATCHPOINTS

- Use a damp cloth or sponge to clean excess adhesive off the tiled surface as you go.
- Tile up to 1 m (1 yd) in height and allow the adhesive to dry before applying any further tiles.
- Once the whole area has been tiled, the battens must be left in place until the adhesive has dried. Once it is dry, remove them and use cut tiles to fill the gaps.

# CUTTING TILES

To complete almost any tile design, you will need to cut some tiles to fill gaps. Cutting a straight line across a tile is relatively easy and you can use one of two tools – either a simple, hand-held tile cutter or a tile-cutting machine. Both will produce the same result.

## SIMPLE CUTTING

**2**

Using a hand-held tile cutter is the most traditional method of cutting tiles. Their simple design combines a handle with a cutting spike that scores the tile as it is drawn across the tile surface. It is worth spending a little extra to get a good quality tile cutter as these produce the cleanest cuts.

1 Measure the distance between the edge of the tile and the corner junction to determine the size of tile needed to fill the gap. Take 3 mm (⅛ in) off the measurement to allow for grout.

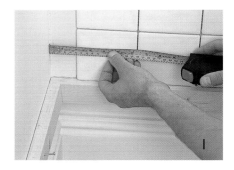

2 Mark the measurement on a full tile with a felt-tip pen. Using another tile as a straight edge, score along the marked line with the tile cutter, applying a firm but even pressure. This will cut into the glazed surface of the tile, leaving a clearly defined scratch.

3 Place the scored tile on two matchsticks so that the 'cut' line is positioned on the centre of each matchstick. Apply even downward pressure either side of the scored line in order to snap the tile along the 'cut' line.

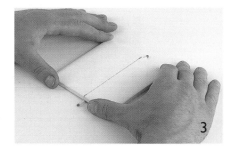

# MACHINE CUTTING

Tile-cutting machines are a more recent innovation. Although they produce the same result as a hand-held tile cutter, they tend to be quicker to use and, with practice, are generally a more efficient way of cutting tiles. The same 'scoring' principle is used, except the cutting blade is circular rather than a single cutting point.

1

2

1  With a felt-tip pen, mark where the cut is required and position the tile on the cutting machine so that the cutting wheel sits directly on the felt-tip line when lowered onto the tile. Applying an even, downward pressure on the machine handle, push the cutting wheel along the full extent of the felt-tip line, scratching the tile surface.

2  Clamp the tile between the bracket above the cutting wheel and below the two sliding rails. The scored line on the tile must be positioned centrally between the rails – most machines have a pointer on the cutting machine bracket so you can line it up accurately. Push down on the cutting machine handle to snap the tile along the scored line.

3

3  Most tile cuts will be clean and precise; if there are any rough edges or bumps, they can be removed with a tile file.

# INTERNAL CORNERS

I nternal corners are the most common obstacle when tiling – quite simply, because all rooms have them. If tiles are being laid on more than one wall in a room, you will have to deal with a corner. Corners are quite straightforward as long as you follow a few simple rules.

## SIMPLE CORNERING

If a tiling plan has been worked out correctly (see pages 26-27), when you arrive at an internal corner you will normally require just under, or just over, half a tile to fill the gap between the last full tile and the corner junction. Cutting is straightforward and it is easy to produce a neatly tiled internal corner.

1 It is usually easier to apply the adhesive to the back of a cut tile, rather than the wall, before positioning the tile along the corner junction. Make sure that the factory edge of the tile is jointed next to the column of full tiles, and that the cut edge is running along the corner junction. Continue up the corner junction, filling the gap with more cut tiles.

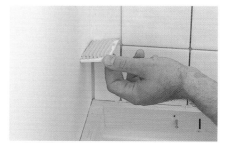

2 Tile the adjacent wall up to the corner junction. This will also need to be finished with a column of cut tiles. It is important to cut these as neatly as possible, as the cut edge of these tiles will overlap the column of tiles on the first wall. Remove any rough edges with a tile file.

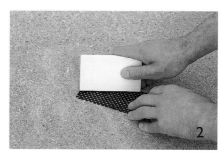

3 Position the cut tiles along the corner junction and continue until the whole internal corner is tiled. Apply adhesive to cut tiles one at a time – don't try and apply it along the entire corner junction.

## KEEPING TILES LEVEL

It is important to keep a constant check that tiles are level when dealing with an internal corner. As cut tiles are just as likely to slip out of position as full tiles, making sure that they stay in the correct place is vital to the overall finish. You need a spirit level and spacers to help you maintain the level across a corner.

1 Check that tiles are in the correct position by holding a spirit level across the corner junction. Position the edge of the level so that one end is at the junction between two tiles on one wall while the other end of the level is positioned on the corresponding row of tiles on the adjacent wall.

2 As you tile, position spacers along the corner so that they span the junction and maintain the necessary gap between, and along, the two columns of cut tiles.

## CUTTING SLIVERS

Sometimes small gaps along a corner will require thin slivers of tile to fill them. Because tiles are brittle, cutting a sliver using the usual cutting technique may break the tile. You need to use a slightly different technique, which puts a greater, more even pressure along the scored cutting line.

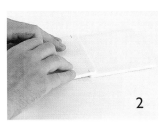

1 Measure off the cut requirements as normal, then score the line with a hand-held cutter or tile cutting machine.

2 Rest the edge of the tile on top of another tile, making sure the scored line is positioned directly above the edge of the tile below. Apply even downward pressure on the main body of the scored tile until the sliver snaps off.

# EXTERNAL CORNERS

Internal corner joins overlap and are easy to conceal, external joins are more prominent and expose any mistakes far more readily. Tiling an external corner is an exercise in concealment, which requires a slightly different tiling technique.

## PLASTIC QUADRANTS

**2**

The greatest aid to producing a neat external corner is the plastic quadrant. It creates a smooth defined edge to tile up to, as well as protecting the corner from being knocked or chipped. Always try to plan your tiling strategy so that full tiles are used to tile away from the external corner.

1 Cut the quadrant to the required length with a hacksaw. Apply adhesive to one wall surface and align the quadrant precisely along the external corner edge. Make sure there is enough adhesive along the edge of the corner to hold the quadrant in position.

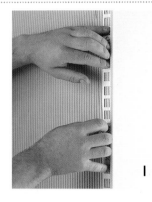

1

2 Tile the one wall, positioning the first tile next to the quadrant, and butting it up tightly against the quadrant lip. Continue to apply tiles. Insert tile spacers along the quadrant/tile junction perpendicular to the tile surface, as the quadrant edge will not allow them to be laid flush against the wall surface (these spacers can be removed when the adhesive dries).

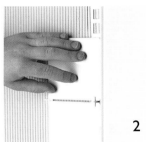

2

3 Once one wall is complete, apply adhesive to the adjacent wall and continue to tile the second wall in the same way.

3

## STANDARD OVERLAPPING

For a more traditional finish when tiling an external corner, you can make an overlapping tile join. Tiles with a glazed edge (as shown here) will maintain the tile colour along the corner; tiles with an unglazed edge can be used for a more rustic finish.

**Creating the junction:** tile the first wall so that the edges of the tiles run precisely along the corner junction. When tiling the adjacent wall, allow the tiles to overlap onto the edges of those previously laid, creating a tiled external corner.

## CREATING CURVES

Ceramic quadrant tiles can be used to create a more curved, smoother edge to an external corner. These are particularly suitable around window reveals, where the external corners run horizontally as well as vertically. Ceramic quadrant tiles give an attractive finish to a window sill.

1   Tile the wall up to the edge of the sill. Use some old broken tiles to build up the actual sill surface, to allow for the height of the quadrant tiles when they are applied. Make sure the broken tiles are stuck down firmly, and provide a level surface.

2   Apply the finishing tiles on top of the broken tile base, positioning them so that they are set back from the sill edge. The distance they are set back should be the same as the width of the quadrant tiles being used.

3   Carefully position quadrant tiles along the sill edge, maintaining gaps with spacers as usual. You may need to apply more adhesive than usual to the back of each quadrant tile to hold them firmly in place.

# GROUTING AND POLISHING

O nce the tile adhesive has dried, you need to fill in the junctions between the tiles with grout to make the tiled surface water-resistant. As well as being practical, grout provides the overall finish, effectively framing the tiles and highlighting their decorative appeal.

**2**

## APPLYING GROUT

Grout can be bought either ready-mixed, or as a powder that needs to be mixed with water. Both will produce the same result, although it is usually more economical to buy the powdered form.

1 Mix grout in a clean bucket with cold water. Proportions will vary between manufacturers, but try to achieve a smooth, workable paste. It is easier to break up any lumps in the mixture if you mix the grout by hand. Always wear protective gloves as prolonged exposure to grout can cause skin irritation.

2 Apply the grout to the tiled surface using a grout spreader or squeegee. Use broad, sweeping movements in all directions to ensure that the grout gets into every joint. Only grout 1-2 sq m (1-2 sq yd) at a time, as there is a fairly short working time before it starts to go hard and it can be tricky to remove grout from the surface of the tiles once it has dried.

3 Remove the excess grout from the tiles with a damp sponge. Build up a rhythm of wiping down tiles and rinsing the sponge in clean water. Continue until all the grout is removed from the surface of the tiles, leaving just the grout in the junctions between the tiles.

4 Run the rounded end of a grout shaper along all the tile junctions. This will give the grout a final smooth surface, making each grouted joint into a perfect, slightly concave trough.

## FINISHING OFF

Once the grout has dried, you need to check to make sure that the surface is watertight and that there are no grout splashes. It is almost inevitable that the odd area will need some minor attention, or that some grout will have found its way onto the tiled surface.

1 As the grout dries, air bubbles inside it come to the surface and create a hole. If this happens, use the end of your finger to apply a small amount of grout to the hole to make the junction waterproof again.

2 Dried grout on the tiled surface can be removed using a window scraper, but take care not to scratch the ceramic surface of the tile with the sharp edge of the scraper. Slide the scraper along the surface of the tile, rather than dig down into it.

3 Finally, polish the tiles with a dry cotton cloth to remove any powdery residue created by the wet grout being applied. You may need to do this two or three times on each area of tiles to remove all the residue and leave a clean, bright surface.

# SILICONE SEALING

A tiled surface is very rigid so any slight structural movement within a room, or building as a whole, can cause joint cracking. Grout is flexible enough to withstand this movement on flat open tiled surfaces, but in corners and more specifically around fixtures such as baths and basins, a more flexible waterproof seal is required. Here, the best thing to use is waterproof silicone sealant, which is sold in tubes.

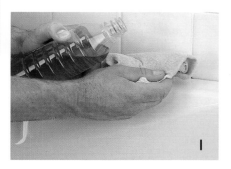

1 To seal between the tiles and the bath, clean the junction of the tiled edge and the bath with some methylated spirits to remove any surface impurities on the bath edge. It evaporates quickly to provide a totally clean surface for the silicone.

2 Apply masking tape along the extent of both the bath edge and the tiled surface, making sure that the tape is stuck down along its entire length. Leave the joint of the tile/bath junction exposed.

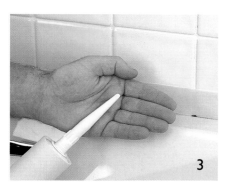

3 Cut off the end of a tube of silicone so that the diameter of the hole will span the joint size created between the two lengths of masking tape. Cut the hole at a slightly sheared angle – this will allow it to be drawn smoothly along the tile/bath junction.

**2**

4 Fit the tube of silicone into a sealant dispenser. Applying even pressure on the trigger of the sealant dispenser, draw the cut end of the tube along the tile/bath junction between the two strips of masking tape. Create a bead of sealant large enough to just cover the edges of the masking tape strips.

5 With a dampened finger, carefully smooth across the surface of the bead of silicone in one continuous, steady motion.

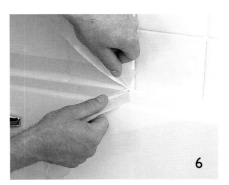

6 While the silicone is still wet, carefully remove the tape to leave a neat siliconed joint. If any area of the joint pulls away as the tape is removed, carefully smooth the silicone back in position with a dampened finger.

## ALTERNATIVE SEALS

Although silicone sealant in a tube is the most commonly used and versatile system of waterproofing a joint, there are other alternatives.

- Sealant dispensers: silicone sealants in a range of colours to match the most common bathroom suites are available in syringe-like dispensers.
- Quadrant tiles: these can be applied along a tile/fitting junction, using silicone sealant as the adhesive to fix them in place (see page 55).
- Plastic sealant strips: these are applied to a tile/fitting junction using double-sided waterproof tape.
- Wooden strips: as long as the wood has had several coats of varnish, decorative wooden mouldings can be used to seal along a junction, using silicone sealant as the adhesive.

# FUNCTIONAL TILES

There is a range of functional tiles available that produce more than just a hard-wearing decorative surface. Applying these tiles requires little more than the basic techniques outlined in this chapter.

**2**

Mirror tiles: as their name suggests, mirror tiles provide the dual function of a tiled surface with the normal properties of a mirror. They are ideal in bedrooms or bathrooms and can be used in small areas – as a splashback for example – or to cover larger areas of wall and create an expansive effect. You can apply mirror tiles in the same way as wall tiles except that you will need to butt them tightly against each other (with no spacers) for the best effect. Some manufacturers recommend their own adhesive for attaching the tiles to the wall.

Worktops: a tiled kitchen worktop is a popular alternative to a veneered or wooden finish. Heat-resistant tiles can be used to provide an area where you can place hot pots and pans from the cooker. Ordinary ceramic tiles are no good for this purpose. Fix the tiles with normal adhesive, but use epoxy grout to finish, as it is more hygienic and hard-wearing.

Soap dish tiles: these tiles have a soap dish fitted in them. They are top heavy compared to a normal tile and need to be supported with masking tape while adhesive dries.

# Tiling Awkward Areas

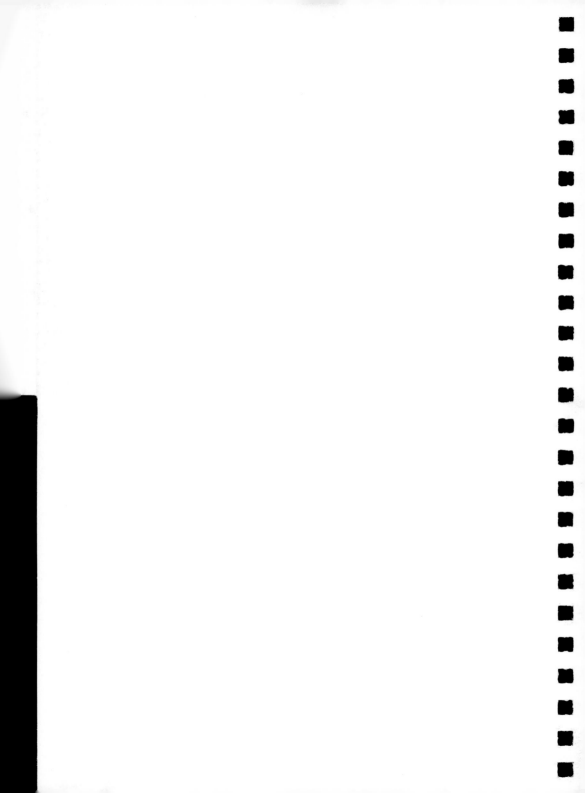

# TILING AWKWARD AREAS

*Once the tiling basics have been mastered and a slightly more complicated tiling project is planned, it soon becomes apparent that most rooms have more than just flat walls and simple corners to deal with. This chapter shows you how to cope with the most common awkward areas found on wall surfaces and explains the easiest and most efficient methods of dealing with them. However daunting some surfaces may appear to be, the same basic rules apply, with the emphasis on cutting tiles accurately and keeping them level. Patience and taking your time is the key to success – speed will come with experience.*

3

# CUTTING AROUND ELECTRICAL FITTINGS

E lectrical fixtures and fittings are the most common obstacles when tiling in kitchens, where power points are required above the worktops to supply household electrical appliances. However, wall lights, switches and other electrical sockets can be found in all manner of places in the house and it is important to use the correct techniques to deal with them.

## WALL FITTINGS

Tiling around fittings such as wall lights cannot be done while they are in position. The best method is to remove the fitting from the wall, leaving the supply wire as the only obstacle. Remember to make sure that the electricity is turned off at the consumer unit before removing the fitting. Draw a wire plan on a piece of paper, so that you can attach the fitting to the wall supply again once tiling is complete.

1 Tape up the end of the supply wire using electrical tape. This will protect the wire and prevent it splaying out, which would make it difficult to thread through the drilled tile later on.

2 Measure the exact point at which a hole is needed in the tile to thread the supply wire through. Holding the tile firmly on the workbench, use a tile drill bit to make a small hole, and then change to a masonry bit to expand the diameter of the hole until it is large enough to accommodate the supply wire.

3 Check that the wire threads through the tile before applying adhesive and fixing it to the wall. Once the surrounding tiles have been applied, remove the tape from the wire. The electrical fitting can now be rewired and repositioned on the tiled surface. Do not turn the electricity back on until the fitting is safely fixed in place.

## SOCKETS AND SWITCHES

Wall-mounted sockets and switches do not need to be completely removed from the wall for you to tile around them. But you must turn off the electricity supply at the consumer unit as the socket plate will need to be loosened by unscrewing the two retaining screws.

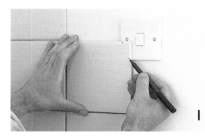

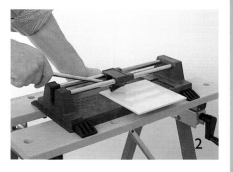

1 Hold a full tile in position over the face of the socket plate. Mark off the portion of tile that needs to be removed, adjusting your measurement so that it appears to encroach onto the socket plate by about 3 mm (⅛ in).

2 Score along the longer of the measured lines with a tile cutter, taking care not to extend the cut any further than the junction with the shorter line.

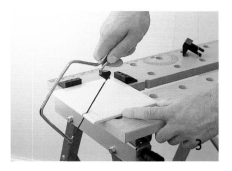

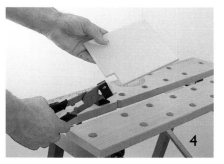

3 Use a tile saw to cut along the shorter line, back as far as the junction with the longer line.

> **CAUTION**
>
> Always turn off the electricity supply at the consumer unit before working around electrical fittings. If in any doubt, contact a qualified electrician to carry out the work.

4 Break off the small portion of tile by applying an even pressure along the scored line with a score-and-snap tool. Loosen the retaining screws on the socket plate and position the tile with the cut edges behind the socket plate to give a neat finish. Refix the socket plate, using slightly longer screws, if necessary, as the depth of the tile may not allow the original screws to reach their previous fixing point.

# CUTTING AROUND PIPES

P ipes are a common problem when tiling. The ideal solution is to box them in before tiling (see pages 22-23), but this is not always possible. Pipes that are left exposed need to be dealt with in as simple a manner as possible. Although pipes may appear to be a daunting obstacle, accurate measuring and cutting are the only skills required.

## MEASURING THE CUT

Pipes are easiest to deal with when they span the junction of two tiles (as shown here), even though this means that two tiles need to be cut. It is important to be very precise when measuring around pipes as there is little room for error and any mistakes will be noticeable.

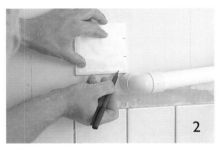

1 Hold the tile to the side and up against the pipe, and mark off the diameter of the pipe on the edge of the tile. Make sure that the tile is held in the right position to allow for the correct spacing with the row of tiles below.

2 To find how far the horizontal cut on the tile will need to be, hold the tile above the pipe, making sure that the vertical edges of the tile are aligned with the corresponding edges in the row of tiles below. Mark off how far the edge of the pipe extends onto the tile.

3 Continue all three markings on the tile to produce a rectangular portion on the pipe side of the tile. Hold a cut-off section of pipe so that it fills the area as completely as possible, without crossing the three marked lines. Draw around the edge of the pipe to produce a perfect guideline for cutting. If no cut off sections of pipe are available, use a compass set to produce the same diameter as the pipe.

## CUTTING

The curve of the portion of tile that needs removing before the tile can be fitted around the pipe makes it impossible to use a tile cutter. A tile saw is the ideal tool for cutting curves.

1 Clamp the tile securely in the workbench and carefully saw around the curve, taking care to keep to the guideline. Once you have reached halfway around the curve, start sawing again from the other end of the curve until the two sawn cuts meet and the unwanted portion of tile is removed.

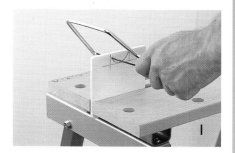

2 Use the curved face of a tile file to remove any rough edges from the cut section of tile.

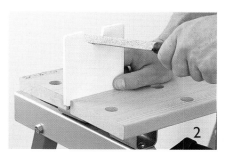

3 Apply adhesive to the back of the tile and position it around the pipe. Repeat the process to fit the adjacent tile around the other side of the pipe.

### CUTTING ALTERNATIVES

• When a pipe is in a position to protrude through a single tile, measure as before, but score and snap the tile through the centre of the marked hole before using the tile saw. Saw the two semi-circular areas and reunite the two halves of tile around the pipe. The cut will not be obvious across the surface as a whole.
• For small pipes, it may be easier to use a large drill bit to form the circular cut for the pipe.
• Use a profile gauge – a tool for copying the shapes of objects – to determine the required shape to cut out of a tile.

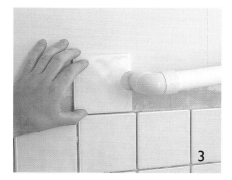

# INTERNAL
# WINDOW REVEALS

R ecessed windows present more of a planning problem than a
cutting problem when tiling. On walls that have a window, it
is essential to try and keep a balanced layout, especially when using
patterned tiles. A little extra time spent planning with a tile gauge
will be beneficial to the overall finish of the room.

## TILING THE WALL FACE

Try and plan the tile layout so that it is central to the window as a whole.
That way any necessary cuts are balanced and are the same size on either side
of the reveal. It is unlikely that the window dimensions will allow for whole
tiles to fit exactly around its border so you will need to cut some tiles. Tiles at
the top edge of the window reveal will also require temporary support with a
wooden batten while the adhesive dries.

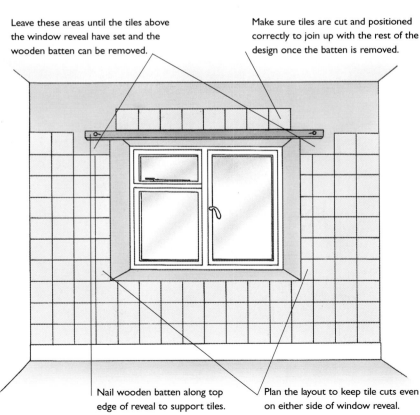

Leave these areas until the tiles above
the window reveal have set and the
wooden batten can be removed.

Make sure tiles are cut and positioned
correctly to join up with the rest of the
design once the batten is removed.

Nail wooden batten along top
edge of reveal to support tiles.

Plan the layout to keep tile cuts even
on either side of window reveal.

## TILING THE REVEAL

Once the wall face is complete, the window reveal can be tiled. Always work back from the edge of the reveal towards the window, so that the cut tiles butt up against the window frame. Tile the top of the reveal first, so that wooden battens can be used to support the tiles while the adhesive dries. If the sill was tiled first, the base of the supporting battens might damage tiles laid on the sill. Tile the sill next, then tile the reveal sides after the sill has dried.

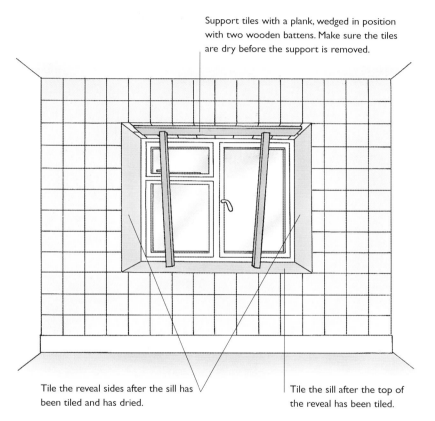

Support tiles with a plank, wedged in position with two wooden battens. Make sure the tiles are dry before the support is removed.

Tile the reveal sides after the sill has been tiled and has dried.

Tile the sill after the top of the reveal has been tiled.

3

**Laying the reveal tiles:** position the tiles in the reveal so that they slightly overlap those on the wall surface. Alternatively, create a rounded edge using quadrant tiles (see page 37).

# MAKING AND TILING A BATH PANEL

Tiling a bath panel has the effect of integrating the bath into the rest of a tiled scheme. As well as their decorative appeal, tiled bath panels make easily wipeable, hard-wearing surfaces, which are totally suited to such a busy area of the home. Use MDF to make the panel itself – it is easy to cut down to size and provides an excellent base on which to apply the tiles.

## MAKING THE FRAME

A bath panel must be built onto a strong frame, otherwise the panel will have too much flexibility, which may cause cracking along tile joints and ruin the finish. Use a framework of 5 x 2.5 cm (2 x 1 in) wooden battens to make a solid base for attaching the panel to.

1 Cut a piece of batten the same length as the bath. Position it on the floor parallel with the bath rim. Hold a cut-off piece of MDF (the same height as the bath panel will be) running from underneath the bath rim down to the floor batten. Use a level to make sure the MDF is vertical, and mark along the edge of the batten making a pencil guideline on the floor.

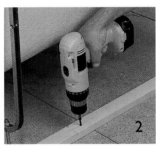

2 Position the wooden batten along the pencil guideline and screw it into the floor. Make sure that the screws are long enough to fix firmly in the floor, but do not go all the way through the floorboard and risk damaging service pipes or wires below floor level.

3 Cut shorter lengths of batten to act as vertical supports, and fix them securely at their base with an angled screw fixing. Most bath designs will accommodate the batten beneath the bath rim, although in some cases it may be necessary to fit another length of batten under the rim to attach to the vertical supports.

4 Finally, fit diagonal supports to make the frame totally rigid. Take care when measuring the lengths required, as you will need to mitre the ends of the battens to ensure that they sit flush against the vertical supports.

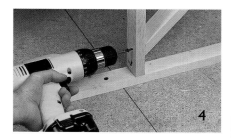

## MAKING THE PANEL

A well-fitting bath panel should create a good decorative effect, so it is important to take your time cutting the MDF sheet to size. Some bath rims have a slightly undulating profile, and this must be taken into account when measuring the MDF.

1 Take precise measurements from under the rim to the floor surface, all the way along the bath. Use these measurements to cut the MDF to size. Fit the panel under the rim, and run a pencil along the edge of the rim, making a guideline on the MDF panel.

2 Remove the panel and lay it flat on the floor. Lay out the dry tiles on the MDF. Do not tile above the pencil guideline or the panel will not fit under the rim when it has been tiled. Once the tiles have been laid out, they can be stuck down with adhesive. Attach the panel to the frame using magnetic catches, or screw it into the battened frame using a tile drill bit and mirror screws.

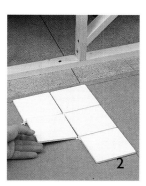

A PATTERNED PANEL
For a unique bathroom feature, use patterned tiles to create your own colour combinations and design.

# TILING AROUND BASINS

B asins tend to have curves and straight edges, which can create problems when tiling around them. The easiest solution is to ease the basin away from the wall and tile behind it. If this is not possible, you can make a paper template of the shape of the basin.

## 'MOVABLE' BASINS

Because basins are plumbed into the mains water supply they cannot simply be moved out of the way before tiling. However, in some cases it is possible to ease the basin away from the wall slightly. You can then slide tiles behind the basin without the need for complicated tile cutting.

1

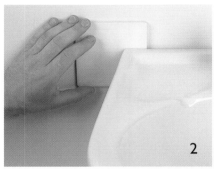

2

1 Most basins are fixed to the wall with retaining screws. Carefully loosen these screws with two or three turns of a screwdriver. Make sure that the basin remains well supported on its pedestal.

2 To check that the basin has been moved far enough away from the wall, try sliding a tile between the back of the basin and the wall. If there is room, it is now simple to tile around the basin. Slip the edge of tiles behind the basin rim to give an extremely neat finish. Once tiling is complete, the retaining screws can be tightened to fix the basin securely in place once more.

### CAUTION

Pipework below basins can be very rigid: easing a basin away from the wall can put joints under stress and risk rupturing them. If in any doubt, do not try this method of tiling around a basin, but use the method shown opposite.

# MAKING A TEMPLATE

Using a paper template is an effective way of cutting tiles around curved edges, such as those found on basins. Cut a number of pieces of paper to the exact size of one of the tiles.

I Using scissors, cut a number of slits along the edge of a paper template. Hold the template against the side of the basin as if it were a tile, allowing the strips of paper to mould into the shape of the basin. Mark a pencil guideline along the crease created.

2 Cut around the pencil guideline, then place the remainder of the template on a tile. Next, draw the outline of the cutout on the tile with a felt-tip pen.

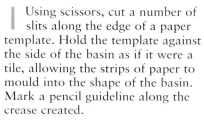

3 Clamp the tile securely on the workbench and saw along the marked guideline. The tile may then be fitted in place next to the basin. Continue to cut and fit tiles around the rest of the basin.

## OTHER AREAS FOR USING A TEMPLATE

- Toilet cisterns: these are often held in position with retaining screws and it may be possible to ease them away from the wall very slightly, as shown on page 52, but proceed with caution and never risk damaging the

pipework. A template can be used just as effectively.
- Shower wall units: if possible, tile before a shower wall unit is fixed. Otherwise, use templates to make the required tile cuts.

# TILING A SPLASHBACK

A splashback above a basin protects the wall from water splashes and is easy to clean. Tiling a splashback is far easier than tiling all the way around a basin, requiring few, if any, cuts. However, it is essential to make sure that a splashback is centralized and maintains a balanced appearance in relation to the basin itself.

## POSITIONING A SPLASHBACK

Decide on the exact dimensions of the splashback. Two to three tiles high is the normal vertical requirement. Along the horizontal line, it is a matter of personal choice – tiles can extend exactly to the basin edge, or protrude further onto the wall surface. This decision may be dictated by tile size, and what looks the most appropriate.

1 Measure the exact centre of the basin, and make a pencil mark on the wall above.

2 Draw a vertical line up from this mark, and use this as a guide to positioning the first tile. Support the tiles on spacers wedged between the tile edge and the basin itself.

3 If the last tile extends farther than the basin edge, support it on a nail hammered into the wall precisely below the bottom edge of the tile.

## FILLING THE GAPS

When tiling a splashback behind a basin, it is essential to make a waterproof seal between the tiles and the basin. Silicone sealant can be used (see pages 40-41). Alternatively, ceramic quadrant tiles can be fitted, using silicone sealant as the adhesive for them.

1 Apply a generous bead of silicone sealant to the back of a quadrant tile along its whole length.

2 Position the quadrant tile at the splashback/basin junction. Continue to apply tiles until the junction is covered. Manufacturers often supply quadrant tiles that are shaped at one end. These give a finished look to the tiles at each end of a splashback junction. Once in place, grout all the tiles.

## FITTING A SURROUND

A tiled splashback can be decorative enough on its own, or a surround can be added to create extra interest. A number of materials can be used for this purpose, it is really a matter of personal preference.

Fitting a hardwood surround: the combination of a hardwood strip against ceramic tiles gives a very attractive finish. Mitre the corners accurately and attach them to the wall with silicone sealant. Varnish the wood to protect it from water splashes before grouting.

# DADOS AND BORDERS

D ados and borders can be used to create decorative edges to tiled designs. As border tiles vary in size and pattern, it is possible to create numerous effects with them. Many designs are made specifically to complement a particular tile design. This means you can follow the manufacturer's lead on creating a design, or you can produce a design of your own choosing.

## TILING A DADO RAIL

Applying border tiles requires the same technique as for standard tiles, except for dealing with corners. These need a slightly different technique, especially when using relief border tiles, as shown here.

1 Apply adhesive to the back of border tiles and then position them on the wall. When a corner is reached, measure the distance from the end of the border tile right into the corner junction.

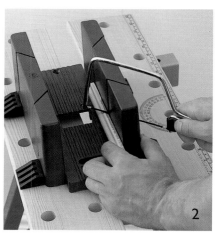

2 Mark off this measurement on a whole border tile. Clamp a mitre block in the workbench and place the marked tile tightly against the mitre block edge. Using a tile saw, cut through the border tile at the mark.

3 Apply adhesive to the back of the mitred border tile and position it in the corner. Not all border tiles will require mitring to go around an internal corner. Mitres are necessary with relief border tiles to produce a good finish: flat border tiles or slips can be given simple straight cuts.

# BORDER CHOICES

As well as complementing a tiled surface, a border can be used in a 'starring' role to create the focus to the entire tiled surface. The look can be traditional or slightly more adventurous. Decisions on the role of border tiles will almost certainly come down to room and surface requirements, combined with the other decorative aspects of the room.

**Half-tile borders:** border tiles are usually between a quarter and half the width of standard tiles. These are the ideal dimensions for using them as a dado rail in a half-tiled room.

**Full-tile borders:** although border tiles are specifically designed for borders, it is not essential to use them when creating a tile divide or border rail. Full tiles of a different design or colour but similar shape to the main body of tiles can be used instead.

**Tile slips:** thin tile slips can be used on their own or as part of a larger overall border design. A multi-level tiled border created out of more than one row of border tiles provides an impressive finish.

# TILING WORKTOPS

Worktops are far easier to tile than wall surfaces, as there are no problems with tiles sliding. The difficulty arises in producing a perfectly flat finish that will be long-lasting as well as hard-wearing. Standard ceramic tiles can be used on a worksurface, but it is better to use tiles specifically designed for worktops as they can withstand hot pans and the general hard wear of a kitchen.

## PREPARING THE EDGE

MDF or marine ply can be used as the worktop base. Whatever is used, the worktop must have a hard-wearing edge – a simple tiled edge is very prone to being knocked and chipped. It is also important to create an edge that is decorative and fits in with the rest of the room scheme. Hardwood bead fitted to the edge protects the tiles and gives an attractive finish.

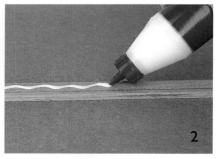

1 Hold a cut strip of wooden bead along the front of the worktop surface (MDF is shown here). Position some tiles up against the edge of the bead so that their faces are flush with the top of the bead. Holding the bead in position, move the tiles away. Draw a line along the back edge of the bead where it meets the worktop surface.

2 Place the bead on the worktop, with the side that has the pencil guideline facing upwards. Apply some wood glue along the bead below the pencil guideline.

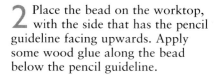

3 Position the bead back on the front of the worktop, making sure that the pencil guideline is still running along the worktop/bead junction. Secure the wooden strip in place with some panel pins.

## APPLYING THE TILES

Once the wooden strip surround is fitted, the tiles may be applied. Always work back from the edge of the worktop towards the wall: that way any cut tiles will be against the wall rather than at the front of the worktop. Use tile adhesive and space the tiles in the usual way.

1 Seal the worktop surface with a PVA solution (five parts water to one part PVA) and allow it to dry.

2 Spread adhesive evenly across the surface of the worktop. The evenness of the adhesive layer is often the secret to producing a level worktop finish, so take time to ensure that it is evenly spread before applying the tiles.

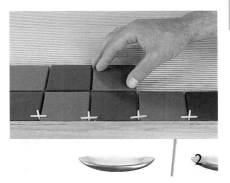

3 Once the tiles have been laid and are dry, finish the tiled surface with an epoxy-based grout. This is more hard-wearing and hygienic than standard grout mixtures. The epoxy grout has a short working time, so only work in a small area at a time, wiping the excess away with a damp sponge as you go.

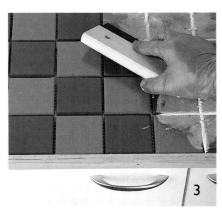

# TILING A FIREPLACE

F ireplaces often form the focal point of a main living area. When tiling a fireplace, there are certain constraints on the type and style of tile you can use. If fitting a new fireplace, tiles made specifically to fit that design are sometimes supplied; when refurbishing a period fireplace, it's often a compromise between authenticity and availability.

1 When fitting tiles on a fireplace, you need to vary the tiling technique by beginning at the top and working down – this makes it easier to centralize the tiles and create a balanced finish with evenly matched cuts where required. Slip the bottom edges of the top row of full tiles behind the metal fireplace surround, so it supports their weight. Make sure the tiles are centralized. Fix a batten on either side of the metal surround to support the tiles that are nearest the edge of the fireplace. If there is no metal surround, nail a batten across the top of the fireplace entrance to act as support.

2 Once these tiles have dried, remove the batten. Tile down to floor level, inserting spacers and making sure the tiles do not slip. The final tile nearest floor level on each side of the fireplace will be supporting the tiles above until they dry, so make sure that these tiles are positioned correctly and supported.

3 Fill in with cut tiles around the edge of the full ones to complete the tiling. Cut some wooden bead to fit around the junction between the tiles and the fireplace to hide the tile cuts. Paint or stain the wooden bead an appropriate colour, then grout the tiles.

FOCAL POINT

A well-tiled fireplace can complement the decoration in the rest of the room, and an attractive set of fireplace tiles makes such a good focal point that the whole colour scheme for the room can be based on the fireplace tiles.

## FIREPLACE CONSIDERATIONS

- Active fireplace: if the fireplace is going to be used, make sure that the tiles are heat-resistant. If surfaces need to be made good before tiling, use fire-resistant cement.
- Finding tiles: to find original tiles, try visiting reclamation yards to see if they save period fireplace tiles – it is often possible to find single replacements for broken originals.

- Be extravagant: because relatively few tiles are needed to tile a fireplace, this is one area where you can use more expensive tiles. A well-chosen set of hand-made or richly patterned tiles are well worth the extra cost.
- Hearths: always consider the hearth when choosing fireplace tiles. It can be an option to continue the tiles from around the fireplace onto the hearth.

3

# INSERTING A MIRROR

**M**irrors make an attractive addition to a tiling scheme, especially when they are framed with border tiles. To make the frame, attach a level supporting batten with masonry nails. Lay the bottom row of tiles along its length. Cut mitres in the tiles so that the top edge of the tiles is the same width as the mirror. Stick them to the wall.

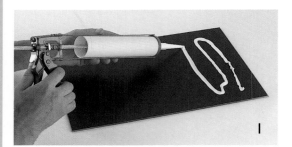

I Apply mirror adhesive across the back of the mirror, spreading it very liberally to ensure that it will be well stuck to the wall surface.

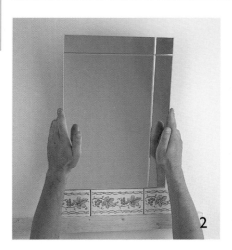

2 Carefully position the mirror on top of the row of border tiles and the supporting batten. Leave until the adhesive on the mirror has dried before applying the rest of the border tiles.

3 Continue applying border tiles around the edge of the mirror until the frame is complete. Try to cut the mitres in each corner so that the cuts correspond to similar areas of pattern. If the border tiles on the sides begin to slip, attach vertical battens to the wall to support them while the adhesive dries.

# Size and Pattern Combinations

### Tiled scenes 64
Make your own scenic pictures on a tiled surface

### Sheet mosaics 66
Use colourful mosaic tiles for an impressive finish in any room

### Broken mosaics 68
Produce an authentic rustic effect with mosaic tiles in random shapes

### Using large tiles 70
Create special effects, such as an natural marble look, with large tiles

### Combining sizes 72
Experiment with patterns and colours using tiles of different sizes

### Diamond pattern 74
Easy and effective ways of varying tile designs

### Brick bond pattern 75
How to produce a minimalist, ordered look on a wall surface

### Herringbone pattern 76
A distinctive pattern for walls or floors

4

# SIZE AND PATTERN COMBINATIONS

*The wide choice of tiles means it is possible to produce all manner of patterns and designs when tiling a surface. In addition to using border tiles to break up uniform tile surfaces, the great variety of shapes and sizes of tiles makes it easy to create designs which do not conform to the traditional appearance of a tiled surface. You can experiment with different-sized tiles to achieve your own very individual look, using tiles uniformly across a wall, or combined with each other to create different patterns and effects. The technique for applying different-sized tiles is basically the same as normal tiles with a few minor modifications.*

4

# TILED SCENES

Tiled scenes are one of the most common uses of specially painted or patterned tiles. They can be used to create a picture or an overall design integrated into the main body of a tiled surface. It is vital to make sure that the scene appears at the right level on the wall. A large tiled scene on an open wall is best positioned at eye level, whereas groupings or smaller scenes can be spread more randomly across the wall surface.

1 Lay out the tiles dry before applying them to the wall, to make sure that you have all the tiles required to complete the design. This also shows you the actual size of the design and helps you work out the best position for it on the wall.

2 Use a coloured grout that complements the main colour in the tiles. This creates a more continuous look, rather than the sharp contrast created by traditional white grout.

4

### TILING ORDER

For some tiled scenes, the tiles will need to be applied to the wall in a specific order in order to produce the finished picture that you want. It is very important to take a little extra time and plan the tiling carefully before applying the tiles.

ADDING CHARACTER
A beautiful tiled scene such as this can combine with the surrounding decoration to add great character to a room, accentuating the room's features as well as providing an attractive focal point.

## DESIGN IDEAS

There are a number of ways in which picture tiles, or complete scenes, can be used to create a decorative finish. It is worth considering different ideas before making a final decision.

- Commission your own scene: many tile firms offer a service whereby your own designs can be reproduced on a tiled scene. Although fairly expensive, this is one way of producing a very individual look.
- Groupings: using a combination of small tiled scenes can be an effective way of adding interest to a large tiled surface.
- Single scene tiles: the occasional single picture tile above a worktop, or surrounding a bath, can enliven a plain finish.

- Using texture: relief tiles are especially effective in a tiled scene, adding an extra dimension to the picture as a whole.
- Framing: simply framing a tiled scene alone on a wall can create an attractive finish. Use wooden beading or border tiles as the frame.
- Tile transfers: these can be applied to plain tiles to create a picture of your own design. This is an inexpensive way of enlivening a plain tiled surface.
- Painting: use ceramic paints to produce your own picture on the tiles. The design need not be complicated, and it is often the most simple brush strokes that create the most dramatic effect.

4

# SHEET MOSAICS

Mosaics can cover entire wall surfaces, or be used in smaller areas, depending on the required effect. As they are so small, mosaic tiles tend to be stuck to a net backing that holds the tiles together in blocks. These blocks or sheets are normally about 30 cm (12 in) square. For tiling the wall, a whole sheet is applied at a time, making progress far quicker than it would be if the tiles had to be applied individually. Some mosaics are covered with a sheet of paper on the tile faces to hold them in position, rather than being backed with netting. This paper is soaked with a damp sponge and removed from the tile surface once the mosaic block has been applied to the wall and the adhesive has dried. The mosaics shown below are the more common type with a net backing.

## APPLYING MOSAICS

Keep sheet mosaics as flat as possible before applying them to the wall, as this makes them easier to pick up and handle. There is no need to use spacers as the individual tiles are held in the correct position by their net backing. Because mosaic sheets are not rigid like a normal tile, they can be difficult to manoeuvre into position. The secret is to begin by applying the bottom of a sheet to the wall first and work upwards to the top row of tiles on the sheet. Because the sheet is made up of so many small tiles, it can be difficult to apply even hand pressure to all the tiles. To make sure they are firmly stuck down, run a mini paint roller backwards and forwards over the mosaic surface, creating an even pressure to bed the tiles into the adhesive below.

4

1 Apply adhesive to the wall before unrolling the mosaic sheets onto it. Apply the bottom of a sheet to the wall first and work upwards to the top row of tiles on the sheet.

2 Run a mini paint roller over the surface of the mosaic tiles, rolling it backwards and forwards with an even pressure to bed the tiles into the adhesive below.

# CUTTING AND GROUTING

Sheet mosaics can be cut down to size to fill gaps along corners and junctions, though this tends to be a fiddly job. Try to plan a design so that it will not involve cutting the tiles themselves – mosaic tiles are so small it is difficult to cut them.

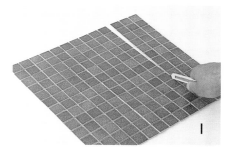

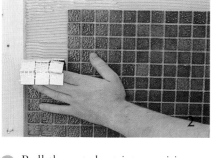

1 Measure the number of tiles required to fill the gap, then cut through the net backing of a mosaic sheet, using a craft knife. Cut as cleanly as possible, taking care not to tear the netting as this will loosen the tiles.

2 Roll the cut sheet into position, again working from the bottom up. Use the mini paint roller to bed in the tiles and even out the join with the adjacent mosaic sheet.

3 Once the mosaic is complete and the adhesive has dried, grout the tiles. Make sure that the grout gets into every tile junction. Sponge off and polish in the usual way.

COLOURFUL MOSAIC FINISH
Combining a variety of mosaic colours and designs makes an impressive finish in any room setting.

# BROKEN MOSAICS

S heet mosaics are designed to speed up the way in which a mosaic can be completed and produce a very even, uniform finish. A more authentic, rustic effect can be produced by using single, randomly shaped mosaic tiles. Applying these tiles is time consuming, but the technique can be used in small areas to make a pictorial design to stick on the wall on its own, or amalgamate into a larger tiled surface. Single mosaic tiles are sold in bags containing a wide range of colours and sometimes different textures. However, you can easily make your own mosaic tiles from old or broken tiles.

**4**

1 To make a small mosaic picture, cut a sheet of thin marine ply to size. Draw a design on it with a pencil, or trace a design onto it from a book.

2 Place some old tiles in a bag or wrap them in a cotton cloth. Strike firmly with a hammer to break up the tiles. Although the bag should stop any splinters of tile flying about, wear goggles to protect your eyes.

3 For more uniform mosaic tiles, cut small sections out of larger tiles with a score and snap tool.

4 Apply adhesive to the tiles one at a time, using a filler knife or scraper. Position the tiles on the design, ensuring that they are firmly stuck in position.

5 Vary the colour and pattern to build up the finished picture. Try and keep uniform gaps between the tiles to allow for grouting.

5

NATURAL EFFECT
A mosaic of broken tile fragments on the wall surface adds a natural effect to an otherwise formal room. The mosaic can complement the colours of furniture and fittings, or provide a complete contrast.

4

## DESIGN IDEAS

As you can create mosaics in all sorts of shapes and sizes, the rules for making them are fairly vague. However, the following guidelines will help you to produce the best possible finish.

- Thickness: try to use tiles of the same thickness – this makes it much easier to produce a mosaic with a flat finish.
- Using other materials: add interest by using different materials within the mosaic – ceramic tiles, broken china and coloured glass can be added to the tiled design. Take care when applying these, and don't leave any sharp edges protruding from the mosaic surface.
- Keeping it simple: the most effective mosaics tend to be those with simple, unfussy designs. Do not be too extravagant when drawing the initial plan.
- Using borders: tiled or wooden borders make excellent frames for a finished mosaic and turn it into a design feature.

# USING LARGE TILES

When applying larger than standard tiles, accuracy is essential because any mistakes are magnified by the size of the tile. The same adhesive can be used, along with standard spacers in most cases. Keeping tiles level and cutting very precisely are vital for a good finish.

## LARGE TILE IDEAS

- Avoid uneven walls: large tiles will accentuate the lumps and bumps in uneven walls. Instead, opt for smaller tiles that 'mould' around any undulations more effectively and give a better result.
- Hire a tile cutter: because larger tiles are sometimes thicker, they can be difficult to cut with standard tile cutters. It may be worth hiring an electrically operated tile cutter from a local retail outlet. These can cut through most tiles very accurately. Follow the manufacturer's operating instructions carefully and wear all the recommended safety equipment, such as protective goggles and gloves.
- Covering large areas: large tiles are ideal for wide open expanses of wall as they cover the area very quickly.

- Tile gauges: when tiling with rectangular tiles, use two tile gauges for planning the layout. One needs to account for tile height, while the other deals with width.
- Avoid intricate areas: don't use large tiles in areas that require a lot of intricate cutting. Marking off accurate curved cuts is always a tricky task, and is even more difficult when using larger tiles.
- Tiling floors: large tiles are usually associated with walls rather than floors, but it is worth considering continuing the tiles from the walls onto the floor surface. Check with your supplier to see if the tiles are suitable for floor use; if they are not, try and find some similar tiles. (See Chapter 5 for floor tiling technique.)
- Allow extra drying time: adhesive under large tiles tends to take longer to dry out than it does under small tiles, so leave supporting battens in place long enough for it to dry properly.

4

## MARBLE TILES

Marble tiles produce a special effect by attempting to create the look of a natural surface, rather than the manufactured appearance of normal ceramic tiles. They are applied to the wall in a slightly different way from any other type of tile. Card is used instead of tile spacers to give a narrow grout joint between tiles, adding to the effect of a totally uninterrupted marble surface.

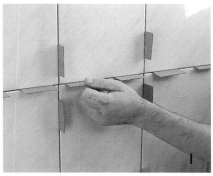

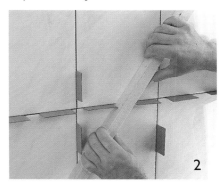

1 Apply marble tiles to the wall using normal adhesive, but use thin pieces of card to space the tiles. Remove the card spacers once the adhesive has dried.

2 After each block of tiles has been applied, hold a wooden batten across the surface to check that all the tiles are sitting flush. Adjust any before the adhesive dries.

LUXURY FINISH
A completely marble tiled bathroom is both stylish and luxurious.

**4**

### MARBLE TILE IDEAS

- Always use an electrically operated tile cutter on marble tiles (see page 70).
- Mitre external corner joins to produce a crisp marble edge.
- Use silicone carbide paper to sand any cuts that are not perfectly smooth.
- The attractiveness of a marble tiled surface depends on it being flat, so it is important to check that the tiles are sitting flush before the adhesive dries.

# COMBINING SIZES

U sing tiles of different sizes within a design allows you to try experimenting with all sorts of patterns and colours. Some manufacturers make different-sized tiles that are designed specifically to be used with one another: small insert tiles, for example, that can be used at the corners of larger, hexagonal tiles. However, it is not necessary to take the lead from the manufacturer, and your own experiments can produce more individual designs.

## DESIGN IDEAS

Simply taking two or three different colours of tile, in two different sizes, allows for numerous possibilities when building up a design. Make sure that the dimensions of the small tiles divide into the dimensions of the large tiles, otherwise it will be difficult to create a pattern.

**Simple rows:** alternating rows of large tiles with rows of small tiles creates a simple but extremely effective design. Alternating the colours as well adds extra interest.

**Chequer-boards:** arranging large tiles with groups of four smaller ones creates a lively variation on the standard chequer-board theme.

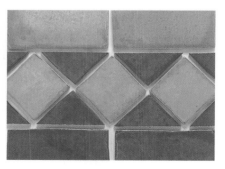

**Diamonds:** a diamond-shaped border running through the main body of larger tiles requires more cutting than the other designs, but is well worth all the extra effort when the tiling pattern is complete.

4

## PLANNING

Once the design has been chosen, planning the actual tile application is important. A more extensive wall plan than usual is required, as it saves a great deal of time if the tiles are positioned in the correct place first time.

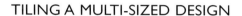

**Drawing the design:** draw a scaled-down version of the design on graph paper, showing colours, shapes and appropriate spacing of the tiles.

## TILING A MULTI-SIZED DESIGN

It is important to be methodical and have an ordered approach while applying tiles in a multi-sized design. When tackling more intricate areas, it is often easier to apply adhesive to the back of tiles and position them singly, rather than applying adhesive to large areas of the wall at a time and then rushing the tile application before the adhesive dries.

1 Attach supporting battens and apply the larger tiles in the usual way, following your design plan.

2 Gradually build up the smaller tile design, using plenty of spacers to maintain the gaps. Keep a constant check on the tiles to make sure that none have slipped.

3 Once the pattern is finished and the adhesive has dried, remove the supporting battens and fill in the edges of the design.

4

# DIAMOND PATTERN

Making a diamond pattern is an easy and effective way of varying a tile design. Colour can be kept the same across the entire surface or two or more colours can be used. Whichever look you prefer, the tiles are applied in the same way although there is some variation from the standard tiling procedure. Starting off correctly is essential – the first tile forms the starting point for the entire design, and mistakes at the base will be accentuated as more tiles are applied up the wall. The vertical batten provides a vital support, as it prevents tiles slipping sideways as rows are built up.

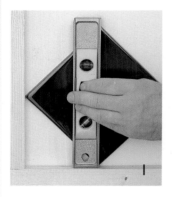

**4**

1 Attach the supporting battens. Use a torpedo level to make sure that the first tile is exactly vertical.

2 Gradually build up the tile levels, ensuring the overall level is maintained. Once the main body of tiles have dried, remove the battens and then use cut tiles to fill the gaps.

STRIKING PATTERNS
A diamond-pattern tile design has a dramatic effect in any room, adding character and interest to surfaces.

# BRICK BOND PATTERN

B rick bond patterns, as their name suggests, mimic the staggered look of building blocks or the jointing system of bricks in the structure of a house. Standard square tiles can be used, but rectangular tiles often provide a more authentic look. White or cream tiles provide a wonderfully minimalist finish, suitable for entire wall surfaces or use in smaller, detailed areas. Colours can be used, if preferred. Spacers need to be cut into a 'T' shape to fit into the tile joints.

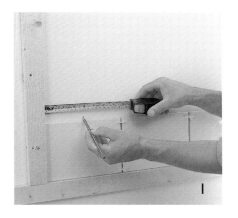

1 Apply the first row of tiles as normal. Measure halfway along the first tile and make a pencil mark on the wall. This gives the position for placing the first tile on the next row to produce the staggered effect.

2 Continue applying rows of tiles, measuring the starting point for each new row as shown in step 1. Once the main body of tiles have dried, remove the battens and use cut tiles to fill the gaps.

4

ORDERED LOOK
Brick bond tiling produces a very ordered look on a wall surface. Here combined with a tile scene, it has been used to create the illusory effect of looking through a window onto the street.

# HERRINGBONE PATTERN

Herringbone patterns, with their very distinctive interlocking blocks, are usually associated with floor tiling or even outdoor driveways. However, their decorative appeal looks equally good inside the home. Rectangular tiles are used to create a herringbone pattern, and, as with brick bond designs, spacers need to be cut into 'T' shapes to fit into the joints. Triangular supports have to be made to support the first row of tiles. These are best made from ply, although any other thin building board can be used.

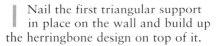

1 Nail the first triangular support in place on the wall and build up the herringbone design on top of it.

2 Continue along the wall surface, interlocking the tiles and adding triangular supports as required. Once the design has been built up, leave the adhesive to dry, then remove the battens and supports. Use cut tiles to fill in around the edges.

**4**

DISTINCTIVE DESIGNS
Once you have mastered the herringbone design, you can go on to create all manner of highly distinctive designs which will dramatically change the tiled surface.

# Tiling Floors

5

# TILING FLOORS

*Tiled floors make an attractive and hard-wearing finish in any area of the home. In many ways, floor tiling is easier than tiling walls – there is less likelihood of tiles slipping out of position. However, it is still vital that tiles are laid correctly to begin with and are not knocked or pushed out of position as the design is built up. As floor tiles tend to be larger and thicker than wall tiles, they are more cumbersome to handle, but practice and experience will soon overcome initial problems. Floor tiles have to be hard-wearing as they will be walked on, and some sound sub-floor preparation is essential.*

# CHOOSING A SCHEME

The choice of floor tiles is immense, and it can be difficult to decide which tiles are best suited to a particular room. Although many decisions will be influenced by the rest of the decoration in the room, when choosing floor tiles remember that they always create a bold statement and become an integral part of the room. It is important to think carefully before you buy floor tiles – they are expensive and will be on the floor a long time.

**Kitchens:** a kitchen benefits from a hard tiled floor as it is easy to clean and very hard-wearing. Edges can be hidden under units, making a professional finish easily achievable. The symmetrical design of a tiled floor such as this also complements the organized feel of a fitted kitchen.

## ADVANTAGES AND DISADVANTAGES OF TILED FLOORS

It is worth weighing up the advantages and disadvantages before deciding on whether or not to lay a tile floor.

**Advantages**
- Highly decorative
- Hard-wearing
- Low maintenance
- Lasts for years
- Easy to clean
- Practical in areas prone to damp

**Disadvantages**
- Often expensive
- Cold underfoot (although underfloor heating is an option)
- Easy for breakages to occur
- Cannot be taken with you when you move house

5

Bathrooms: because bathrooms periodically get damp, a tiled floor makes an ideal surface – carpets are prone to rotting.

## ESTIMATING QUANTITIES

- The simplest way to estimate how many tiles are needed for the job is to multiply the width and length dimensions of the room to get the floor surface area, then divide this figure by the surface area of one tile.
- For irregular rooms, calculations can be slightly more difficult and it may be easier to divide the room into smaller areas.
- Always add between five and ten percent onto the total tile figure to allow for breakages. Cutting round the edges of a room always takes more tiles than expected, as well. It is also useful to have a few tiles to replace any cracked tiles in the future.
- Buy slightly more adhesive than recommended by manufacturers: they often underestimate the amount needed to finish the job.

Other areas: hard tiles need not be confined to just kitchens and bathrooms; they can be used effectively in all areas of the home as their decorative appeal makes them a desirable finish for any room.

5

# PREPARING WOODEN FLOOR SURFACES

W ooden floor surfaces need thorough preparation before tiles can be applied. The floor must be made rigid, as any movement once the tiles are laid will cause the tiles to move and crack the grout joints. The most common way of preparing a wooden floor for tiles is to make good the floorboard surface and lay a ply or chipboard sub-floor as a base for the tiles.

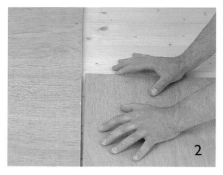

1 Check the entire floor area to see if any boards are loose. Knock in protruding nails with a hammer and punch, and screw down any boards that are not firmly in position.

2 Cover the floor with sheets of ply with a minimum thickness of 18 mm (¾ in). Screw the sheets to the floorboards below, at intervals of 30 cm (12 in) in every direction.

3 Stagger the edges of the sheets of ply, and make sure that the edges are butted up against each other.

### CAUTION

When screwing into the floor surface, make sure that the screws you use are long enough to bite firmly into the floorboards, but not so long that they go beneath the boards and run the risk of damaging any service pipes and wires below floor level.

5

# DEALING WITH FLEXIBILITY

However firmly fixed down a wooden floor may be, there is always a danger that there will still be enough movement to put tile joints under stress. Some manufacturers recommend a specific system for dealing with flexible floors. The best course of action is to use a proprietary flexible floor adhesive for applying the tiles. Alternatively, some manufacturers now supply a proprietary tile sheet that is sandwiched between layers of adhesive and applied as shown below. Available in a variety of shapes and sizes, the sheet can be trimmed to size with a craft knife, if necessary.

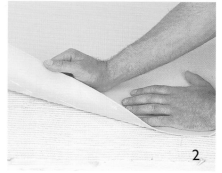

1 Before applying the proprietary tile sheet, brush the sheets of ply with a PVA solution (five parts water to one part PVA) to seal it. Leave the solution to dry.

2 Apply tile adhesive to the floor. Then, while it is still wet, unroll and stick down a proprietary tile sheet on top of the adhesive. Leave it to dry and then apply adhesive over the sheet. Lay the tiles on top, as usual.

## ADJUSTING OTHER LEVELS

Floor tiles raise the floor level, so you may need to consider other areas in the room that may be affected by this change to the floor.

- Doors: you may need to cut a little off the bottom of doors so that they will be able to open onto the newly tiled surface.
- Skirting: shallow skirting board will look even smaller once tiles are applied to the floor. It is often better

to remove the skirting before tiling and then refit it when the floor is finished. This has the added advantage of covering the cuts around the edge of the room.

- Thresholds: as well as adjusting the door, it may be necessary to fit a threshold strip to make a clean dividing step between the tiles in one room and the floor covering in the next room.

5

# PREPARING CONCRETE FLOOR SURFACES

Concrete floor surfaces need less preparation than wooden ones – there is no need to worry about the rigidity of a concrete base, as it is far less prone to movement than wood. The main emphasis is on making sure that the floor is level and clean, and that there are no impurities on the surface that could react with the adhesive and affect its ability to stick the tiles.

## REMOVING OLD FLOOR COVERINGS

It is essential that you take up old floor coverings – carpet, vinyl and other miscellaneous coverings – before applying tiles. The only exception is when there is a well established old tiled floor as a base. These existing tiles must be firmly stuck down and all polish or sealant coatings removed before new tiles can be applied.

1 Use a spade to prise underneath stubborn old linoleum or vinyl flooring that has been glued down. Scrape it away from the concrete surface below.

2 Once all the old flooring has been taken up, remove any remnants of old glue with a scraper. Use a proprietary glue remover to aid this process, if necessary.

3 Brush and thoroughly clean the whole floor. When it is clean, apply one coat of proprietary floor sealer to the entire area and leave it to dry before tiling.

# MAKING GOOD

Years of wear normally take their toll and there will be some areas of an old concrete floor that require extra preparation before tiles can be laid. It is important to fill in any cracks and holes so the entire surface is level. Failure to fill holes will make tiling more difficult and waste adhesive. Dust out holes and dampen them before filling them.

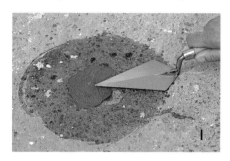

1 Fill large holes with a standard sand and cement mix (one part cement to four parts sand, mixed with water to a stodgy consistency). Smooth the filled area with a trowel.

2 For more undulating floors, it is necessary to return the concrete screed to a level base. Mix up some proprietary self-levelling compound and pour it onto the floor surface.

3 Using a steel float, spread the compound across the entire floor. It will find its own level, gathering more in any depressions in the floor. Once dry, the compound produces a perfectly level finish.

## NEW CONCRETE SCREEDS

With a new concrete screed, a little care has to be taken before tiling, even though the surface may be perfectly level.

- Damp course: the screed must be laid over a damp course membrane, otherwise rising moisture will lift a tiled surface.
- Priming: always seal new screeds with a proprietary sealer.

- Checking dryness: even when a screed appears to be dry, it is worth using a damp meter to check that this is the case. Depending on depth, some screeds can take weeks or even months to dry out fully. Ask your tile supplier what the optimum damp meter reading should be before you use a particular type of tile on a new concrete screed.

5

# WHERE TO START

A s with all tiling projects, it is essential to begin in the right place. No room is completely square, so it is never possible to start in one corner and tile around the room. Instead, you have to find the centre of the room and make your calculations based on this point so that all the cut tiles will be around the edge of the room.

## FINDING THE CENTRE OF A ROOM

Finding the centre of a relatively square or rectangular room is fairly simple. For more awkwardly shaped rooms, the principle of measuring the centre of wall dimensions is still the same.

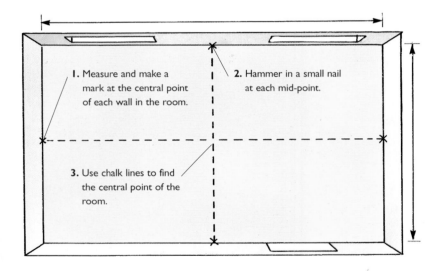

1. Measure and make a mark at the central point of each wall in the room.

2. Hammer in a small nail at each mid-point.

3. Use chalk lines to find the central point of the room.

**Snapping a line:** attach a chalk line between two of the nails on opposite walls. Making sure that it is tight, lift the line above the floor surface, and then let go to allow the line to 'snap' onto the floor. When the line is removed, a chalk impression is left behind to provide a precise guideline across the centre of the room. Attach the line to the other two opposite nails and repeat the process. The second line will bisect the first and thus give the exact central point of the room.

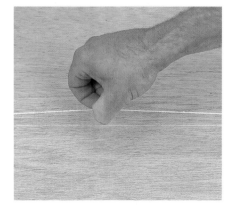

5

## PLANNING THE LAYOUT

The easiest way – laying tiles from the centre of the room outward – can trap the tiler in a corner. The best plan is to use the central line as a guide, and move this guideline towards the wall farthest from the door. Tiles can then be applied continuously towards the door, allowing the tiler to get out of the room without walking on setting tiles.

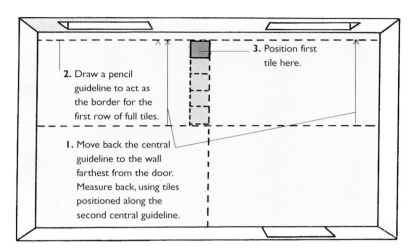

**3.** Position first tile here.

**2.** Draw a pencil guideline to act as the border for the first row of full tiles.

**1.** Move back the central guideline to the wall farthest from the door. Measure back, using tiles positioned along the second central guideline.

**3.** Once the full tiles have dried, fill in around the edge of the room with cut tiles.

**1.** Work away from the first tile towards the far corner of the room. It is often easier to apply two rows of tiles at a time.

**2.** Work away from the other side of the first tile and continue in rows until the door is reached and all the full tiles have been laid.

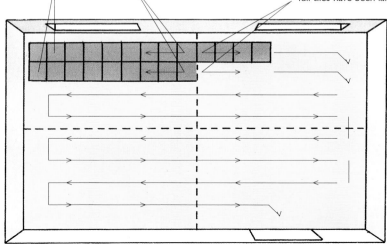

5

# LAYING THE FIRST TILES

B efore laying the first tiles, make sure that all tools are to hand and that the floor surface is free of any obstructions. The first tiles are the cornerstone of the whole floor and must be positioned correctly. Apply adhesive evenly and keep tools, hands and tiles as clean as possible while tiling.

## GUIDELINES

Although a pencil line acts as a good guideline for placing tiles in position, it is very easy to accidentally knock tiles out of position, and this may go unnoticed until the adhesive has dried. It is safer to nail a wooden batten along the pencil guideline, then the first row of tiles can be butted up to this batten.

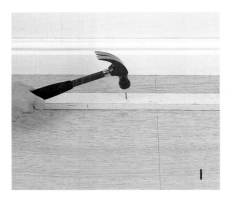

1 Nail a wooden batten along the pencil guideline for the first row of tiles to butt up against.

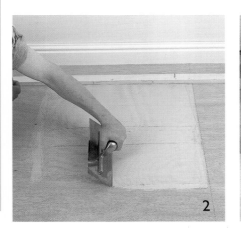

2 Apply adhesive to the floor in areas of 1 sq m (1 sq yd). This should provide enough adhesive coverage for two rows of tiles to be applied at a time.

3 Press the first tile into position tight up against the batten, making sure the tile is also aligned with the central guideline of the opposite wall.

5

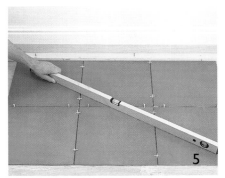

4 Fit spacers perpendicular, or upright, to the tile surface rather than flat on the floor between tiles (see below, right).

5 Once a block of six or more tiles has been laid, check that the tiles are level; adjust adhesive levels if any are sitting proud or have sunk.

6 Sponge the tile surface with clean water as you progress across the floor, to keep it clean and adhesive-free.

### SPACERS

Spacers are fitted perpendicular to the tile surface rather than flat on the floor between tiles so they can be removed when the adhesive is dry. Because the floor surface must be hard-wearing, the grout needs to be as deep as possible. Spacers left in place, reduce the depth of grout and create a weakness.

5

# CUTTING TILES

Floor tiles are cut in the same way as wall tiles with a few minor variations. Use a good quality hand-held tile cutter, or tile-cutting machine, and make sure you measure and cut accurately. If you have a lot of thicker floor tiles to cut, it may be worth hiring an electrically operated tile cutting machine.

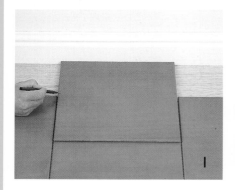

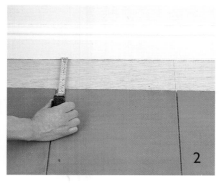

1 Where the tiles and the skirting board run parallel, place the tile to be cut on top of the adjacent tile, butting the edge of it against the skirting board or wall. Mark where it needs to be cut, allowing for spacers and therefore grout.

2 Where the distance between the last full tile and the wall surface is not consistent all the way along the wall, measure the distance with a tape measure and transfer the measurements to the tile before cutting it.

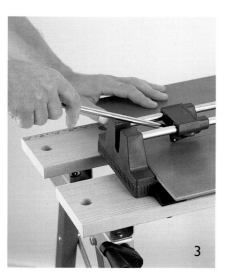

3 Clamp the tile in the tile-cutting machine. Applying downward pressure on the cutting wheel, push it across the tile surface to score it. Position the tile above the cutting wheel and below the sliding rails, and snap down with the machine handle to cut the tile.

5

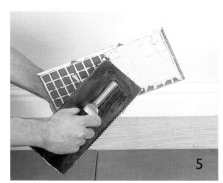

4 Use the tile file to remove any jagged edges along the cut tile. Larger lumps and bumps can be nipped away with tile nibblers.

5 Check that the tile fits the gap before applying adhesive directly to the back of the tile, spreading it in the usual way.

6 Position the cut tile, making sure that the factory edge is jointed with the main body of tiles and the cut edge faces the skirting board or wall. Use spacers in the normal way.

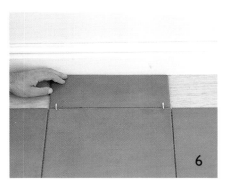

**Using a profile gauge:** this is the ideal tool for producing a precise outline of an intricate area, such as a door architrave. The gauge is adjustable and moulds around any surface. The outline can be transferred onto a tile and used as a guide for cutting with a tile saw.

5

# MAKING TEMPLATES FOR FLOOR TILES

Tiling a floor inevitably involves some intricate cutting. Profile gauges (see page 89) can be used in some areas, but a paper template is often the best way of dealing with awkward areas. Make sure that the tile saw blade is sharp enough to cope with intricate cuts.

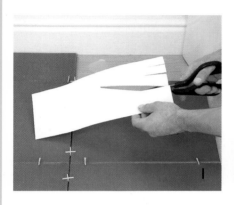

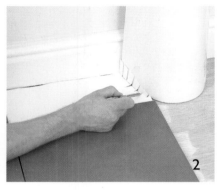

1 Cut a piece of paper to the size of tile needed, as if there were no obstacle to be cut around. Cut several slits along the edge of the paper. Cut more slits for intricate shapes than for simple ones.

2 Position the paper as if it were a tile, allowing the slits to lap up onto the obstacle (a basin pedestal is shown here). Crease the slits along the floor/pedestal junction and mark along the crease with a pencil.

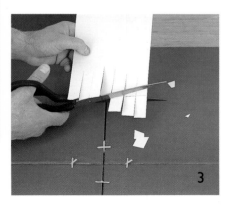

3 Remove the paper, flatten out the slits and then cut along the pencil guideline to produce an exact template of the pedestal profile.

5

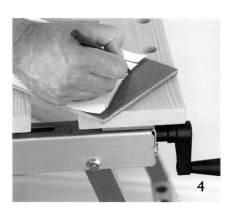

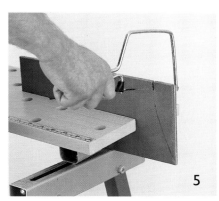

4 Holding the template firmly in position on the tile to be cut, draw along the curve of the template with a felt-tip pen.

5 Clamp the marked tile in the workbench. To prevent the cut portion snapping off before the cut is complete, saw halfway along the felt-tip line then turn the tile and saw the other half. Support the cut part of the tile with your free hand once it nears breaking away.

6 File away any rough edges. Then apply adhesive to the back of the tile and position it next to the pedestal. Insert spacers between the tiles in the usual way.

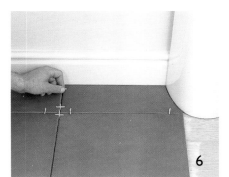

### TEMPLATE GUIDELINES

It is hard work sawing through a floor tile, so always double check the template measurements and the guideline on the tile to make sure that they are correct before you start. For very intricate shapes, it may be necessary to cut more slits in the template so that it can mould accurately around the obstacle.

5

# GROUTING FLOOR TILES

U nglazed tiles must be sealed with a proprietary sealer before grouting, to prevent grout becoming ingrained in the tile surface. However, most tiles are already glazed and grouting can take place as soon as the adhesive has dried. Remove the spacers before grouting. Always use grout that is specifically designed for floors – wall tile grout is not so hard-wearing. Floor grout has a coarser texture, so it is essential that it is well mixed with no dry or lumpy bits.

1 Put the grout in a bucket and gradually add cold water until the mixture is a firm but pliable consistency. Wear protective gloves as prolonged exposure to grout can cause skin irritation.

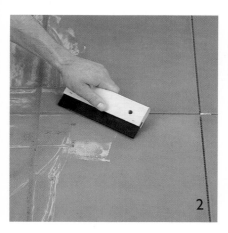

5

2 Apply the grout to the tiles with a grout spreader, working the spreader in all directions across the tile joints to ensure that every joint is filled with grout.

3 Using a damp sponge, wipe away the excess grout from the tiled surface after every few tiles have been grouted – it is much harder to remove grout from tile surfaces when it has dried.

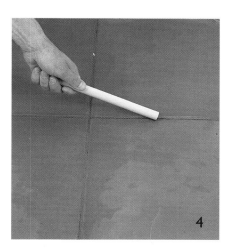

4 Smooth the grout joints with a piece of wooden dowel, making each grouted joint into a concave trough shape. Wipe away excess grout with a damp sponge.

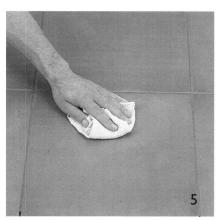

5 Once the grout has dried, polish the tiles with a dry cotton cloth to remove the thin cloudy residue of dilute grout. Each tile will need to be wiped two or three times to remove all the residue.

6 Replace the skirting board if this was removed before tiling the floor. The skirting board will hide the cut edges of the tiles.

## GROUTING COLOUR

Floor grout is supplied in many different colours, so you can choose a suitable grout for the tiles that you are using. It is usually best to use a dark complementary grout colour because light contrasting colours show the dirt more easily, and stains in the grout will be more noticeable. Darker colours tend to be the more hard-wearing option.

5

# LAYING HEAVY-DUTY TILES

A s well as standard floor tiles, there are heavy-duty varieties – the most common of which are quarry tiles. Although smaller in size than most floor tiles, they are considerably thicker and require laying on a bed of sand and cement (mortar), rather than adhesive.

1 Nail a support batten parallel to the wall. Measure out a section to be battened off, using some tiles laid dry and including spacers. Nail in two more battens to section off the area. Remove the tiles.

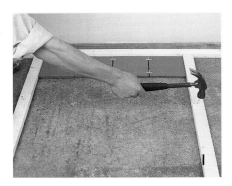

2 Mix the mortar, using four parts sand to one part cement. Stir them together then gradually mix in enough water to make a stodgy consistency.

3 Pour the mortar into the area that is sectioned off with battens and spread it with a trowel, making it as level as possible at a depth of about 12 mm (½ in).

5

4 Lay tiles on the mortar surface and give them a tap with the butt end of a hammer to bed them in firmly. Fit spacers perpendicular to the tile surface so that they are easy to remove when the tiles are dry.

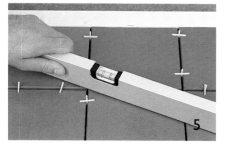

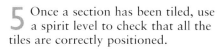

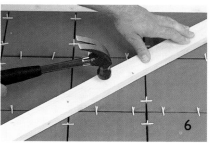

5 Once a section has been tiled, use a spirit level to check that all the tiles are correctly positioned.

6 Hold a piece of batten across the tiled surface and give it one or two taps with a hammer along its length to ensure that the tiles are well bedded in and are level. Leave to dry then remove the battens and spacers before tiling another section. Some tiles will need to be cut to finish around the edge of the room. A standard tile cutter will cut some varieties; however, it is easier to hire an electrically operated tile cutter if the tiles are particularly hard.

## WORKING IN SECTIONS

Once the usual support batten has been nailed parallel to the wall, you need to nail in two further battens at right angles to act as barriers that will prevent the mortar from spreading too far across the floor. Sectioning off areas also makes it much easier to keep the mortar and the tiles level.

5

# GROUTING HEAVY-DUTY TILES

Quarry tiles can be grouted with normal floor tile grout, but heavier flagstones and natural stone tiles need to be grouted with a sand/cement mix (mortar) to create a long-lasting seal. In both cases, the aim is still to fill all joints as neatly as possible.

**Grouting quarry tiles:** follow the normal floor tile procedure and spread the grout across the surface, making sure that it gets into all the joints. Clean off the excess with a damp sponge as you proceed across the floor.

**Grouting flagstones:** use a pointing trowel to press mortar into the gaps between the stones. Gently smooth over the mortar with a paint brush, creating a well-defined edge to the junction between mortar and stone.

**5**

RUSTIC FEEL
Natural stone floors are the most hard-wearing of all floor coverings and give a lovely rustic feel to a room.

# Repair and Renovation

# REPAIR AND RENOVATION

*However well tiled a surface is, it is likely that at some stage you will need to carry out repair work – it is much better to replace a single damaged tile than the whole surface. Also, fixtures may be added or changed, and it is important to know how to deal with the tiles. Old tile surfaces can be renovated and sometimes even the shabbiest of floors can be given a new lease of life. This chapter deals with the many areas related to working on existing tiles, either improving their look or changing their appearance to suit the required need.*

6

# REPLACING DAMAGED TILES

T he most common repair to any tiled surface is replacing a cracked or broken tile. Although tiles have a hard surface, they can be cracked by too much physical abuse. In some cases, they simply have a weakness that causes cracking over time. Replacing a tile is a relatively simple procedure that can be carried out without damaging any of the surrounding tiles.

## REMOVING AN OLD TILE

In some cases, a damaged tile may lift out of place easily. Unfortunately, most of the time they need far more persuasion – although the tile may be broken, the adhesive holding the various pieces is as strong as ever.

1 Loosen the grout around the edge of the cracked tile with a grout raker, running the blade up and down the joint quite vigorously. Take care not to damage the edges of surrounding tiles.

2 Drill a number of small holes across the surface of the broken tile to break up and weaken the entire tile. Wear goggles to protect your eyes from any flying debris.

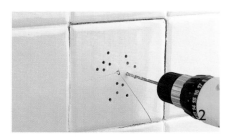

3 Use a hammer and cold chisel to knock out the broken up tile, taking care not to dig the point of the chisel into the wall surface underneath (see below).

### BROKEN PIECES

As broken pieces of tile are gradually removed, it becomes easier to position the chisel in a levering position behind the fragments of tile to remove them. Always wear protective goggles while carrying out this procedure.

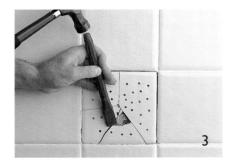

6

## INSERTING THE NEW TILE

Compared with removing broken tiles, inserting a new tile is a relatively simple procedure. Tile replacement is a good reason for keeping a few spare tiles after each new tiling project is finished, rather than trying to buy a matching tile at a later date.

1 Use a scraper to make sure that all the old adhesive and splinters of tile are removed from the wall, leaving a relatively smooth surface for the new tile.

2 Apply adhesive to the back of the new tile and carefully position it in the hole.

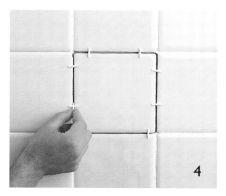

3 Hold a wooden batten across the new tile and the surrounding tile area to check that the new tile is positioned flush with all the other tiles. Adjust the new tile before the adhesive dries, if necessary.

4 Apply spacers perpendicular to the tile surface to maintain the required gap around the new tile. Once the adhesive has dried, remove the spacers and grout around the joints of the replacement tile.

6

# DRILLING TILES

Adding a new fitting to tiles poses the problem of attaching it. Although there are many self-adhesive hanging mechanisms available, by far the most secure system always involves screw fixings and brackets. Drilling into tiles to anchor such screw fixings is a straightforward process as long as the correct procedure is followed.

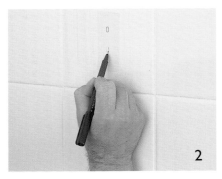

1 Position the fixing bracket in the centre of a tile. Make a mark with a dark coloured felt-tip pen to show the required fixing points, using a level to keep the bracket precisely vertical.

2 Stick a piece of masking tape over the felt-tip pen marks on the tile and redraw the bracket position on the tape. (Masking tapes are usually transparent enough to make this re-marking possible.)

3 Using a tile drill bit, drill holes through the tiles at the felt-tip pen marks. Hold the bit against the tile surface before starting it, to prevent the drill from jumping across the tile. The masking tape prevents the bit from sliding.

6

4 To reduce mess, hold a vacuum cleaner nozzle under the holes to catch the dust that comes out as they are drilled. Red brick or concrete dust could discolour the grout.

5 Remove the masking tape and press a wall plug the same size as the drill bit into each hole – tap them with the butt end of a hammer, if necessary.

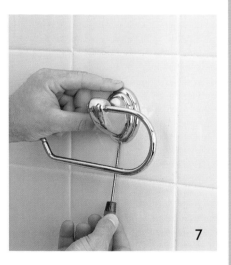

6 Screw in the fixing bracket, checking that it is level. Make sure that the screws bite firmly into the wall plug as they are screwed in.

7 Attach the fitting to the bracket. This usually requires tightening a small grub screw found at the base of the fitting.

### CAUTION

Try to avoid positioning fixings too near the edge of tiles as it spoils the aesthetic look, and drilling near the edge of tiles runs the risk of cracking or chipping them.

6

# CHANGING GROUT

G rout deteriorates over time, becoming stained. To keep the tile surface looking clean and bright, you may need to regrout the tiles at least once during the lifespan of the surface – particularly in areas that are constantly under attack from water, such as shower cubicles and splashbacks.

## REGROUTING

Although regrouting is time consuming, it can totally rejuvenate the tiles and is far more economical than replacing all your tiles. A grout raker is the ideal tool for removing the old grout, or the edge of a scraper can be used.

1 Use the grout raker along all the joints on the tiled surface. Take care not to scratch the edges of tiles, and be sure to remove as much of the old grout as possible.

2 Regrout the whole surface using the normal technique (see pages 38-39), taking care to work the grout into all the joints.

---

### KEEPING GROUT CLEAN

There are a number of ways of lengthening the lifespan of grout.
- Polish the surface with a silicone-based spray. This cleans the tiles as well as sealing the grout, making it much more difficult for water to penetrate it.

- Make sure that bathrooms have extractor fans, so the damp air is not allowed to linger in the room.
- Rinse down the tiles in a shower cubicle after use, and make sure that dripping shower heads or taps are fixed as soon as possible.

6

## CHANGING COLOUR

Grout does not have to be white, and regrouting provides the opportunity to have a colour change. A contrasting colour to the tiles can be used, or, as shown here, a similar colour gives a very even and coordinated surface. Proprietary coloured grouts often have different mixing systems; however, in most cases it is possible to vary the colour intensity of the grout and produce a colour that matches or complements the tiles.

1 Wearing protective gloves, mix up the powdered grout in a bucket, adding enough water to make a smooth creamy consistency.

2 Apply the grout over the entire surface with a grout spreader, taking care to work the grout into all the tile joints.

3 Remove the excess grout from the tiles with a damp sponge. Leave the grout to dry then polish the tiles in the usual way.

6

# MAINTAINING GROUT AND SILICONE

In many cases where the grout is stained, it is possible to perform a general maintenance job, rather than having to undertake a complete replacement of grout. Silicone seals may need renewing if they are discoloured or if the seal has broken and is letting in water.

## CLEANING GROUT

Partially discoloured white grout can often be revived by simple cleaning with a diluted bleach solution. This has the effect of removing dirt and grime, and bringing the grout back to its original colour.

**Using a toothbrush:** apply the diluted bleach solution to the grout with an old toothbrush, scrubbing vigorously along all the joints. Wear protective gloves, and rinse the tiled surface thoroughly with clean water after cleaning with bleach.

## GROUT CLEANING KITS

Small kits produced specifically for cleaning white grout can be used very successfully. These literally paint the grout in order to bring it back to its original bright white finish.

1 Use a fitch to apply the grout cleaning solution along all the tile joints. Leave it on for the time recommended by the manufacturer.

2 Once the grout has dried, remove the excess fluid from the tiled surface with a clean, damp sponge.

# REAPPLYING SILICONE

As well as improving the overall look, reapplying silicone renews the water seal between tiles and other surfaces. Most reapplications are required around basins, in shower cubicles or, as shown here, around the edge of a bath.

1 Using a craft knife, cut away the old silicone seal. Cut into the junction to avoid scratching the surface of the bath.

2 For areas of tough silicone, apply a proprietary solvent and allow it to soak in for the time recommended by the manufacturer.

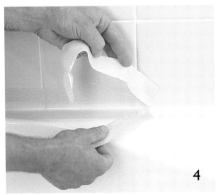

3 Use a window scraper to remove the residue, taking care to keep the blade flat on the bath surface to avoid scratching it.

4 Run masking tape along either side of the junction and then apply a new bead of silicone (see pages 40-41). Remove the tape as soon as the silicone is applied.

6

# RESTORING AN OLD TILED FLOOR

Individual taste and preferences vary greatly, and what suits one person might not suit another. This means it is quite common for people to restore or expose areas within the home that previous owners felt were unattractive – old tiled floor surfaces that have been covered with carpet by one person, for example, provide an ideal restoration project for another.

1 Lift and remove the old carpet. Much of the poor condition of the tiles below the carpet will be due to discolouration or old adhesive and dust from the carpet.

2 Use a scraper to remove any large areas of glue and carpet backing that is partially stuck down. Keep the scraper blade flat with the tile surface to avoid scratching.

3 Wash down the surface with clean water, using wire wool to remove any stubborn areas of dirt or grime. If necessary, use a proprietary tile cleaning solution to remove any ingrained dirt.

4 Finally, run a window scraper along all the grout lines and in any small depressions on the tiled surface to remove the last specks of dust and debris, and ensure the surface is as smooth as possible.

6

5 Clean down the entire surface once more with a mild detergent solution, then rinse thoroughly with clean water. Regrout, if necessary.

6 Apply a proprietary floor sealer to give the cleaned tiles a hard-wearing finish and prepare them for everyday traffic.

RESTORING ORIGINALS
An old, restored tile floor tends to have more character than a newly laid one. Colour variations and time create a greater feeling of texture and authenticity.

6

# REPAIRING A DAMAGED FLOOR

**B**oth old and relatively new floor tiles may need repairing or replacing at some point. As with wall tiles, repairs are relatively simple and far more economical than replacing the entire surface. However, floor tiles are much tougher than wall tiles, and this must be taken into account when doing repairs.

## REPLACING A FLOOR TILE

Floor tiles sometimes crack because they were laid poorly, or there may be a weakness within the tile that can lead to cracking over a period of time. Whatever the cause, a cracked tile needs to be replaced as it is not possible to repair it successfully.

1 To weaken the entire tile, drill a number of holes randomly across its surface. Wear goggles to protect your eyes from any flying debris. Loosen the grout around the edges of the tile with the corner of a scraper.

2 Use a hammer and bolster chisel to break up the tile surface. Do not position the chisel near the edge of the tile or you may damage the surrounding tiles. Remove the broken pieces of tile.

3 Clear any debris before applying the new tile on a fresh bed of adhesive. Use spacers in the joints, and hold a spirit level across the tile to check that it sits flush with the surrounding area. Allow the adhesive to dry, remove the spacers and grout the tile joints.

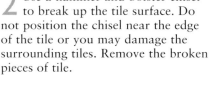

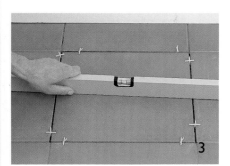

6

## MAKING GOOD DAMAGED AREAS

Small chips or dents don't really warrant full tile replacement – they can be dealt with in a less dramatic manner. Most marks on tiles are superficial and can be wiped away with a proprietary cleaning solution; however, if a heavy item has been dropped on the tile and chipped the surface, some camouflage work is required to hide the damage.

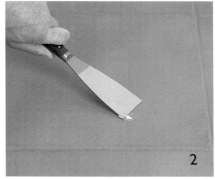

1 Brush away any dust or loose chips from the damaged area of the tile. Blow gently to remove any dust from the bottom of the hole, if necessary.

2 Mix some stainable filler and press it firmly into the hole with a filler knife. Make it as neat as possible so that it does not require sanding once it dries.

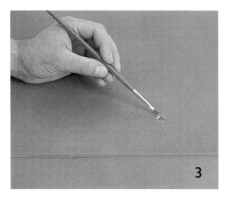

3 When the filler is dry, paint the repaired area with an oil-based paint that matches the surrounding tile colour.

4 Allow the paint to dry then protect the repair by applying some proprietary floor-tile sealant to the immediate area.

6

# RENOVATING SLATE FLOORS

The texture of slate tiles makes them more prone to picking up dirt than the flatter surface of normal ceramic tiles – this means that slate floors require more attention than standard tile floors. From time to time they need rigorous and thorough cleaning in order to maintain the slates in the best condition possible.

1 The ideal tool for cleaning slate tiles is a wallpaper stripper with the broad stripping plate removed to leave just the steam supply pipe. Directing the steam at ingrained areas of dirt aids the removal process and leads to a much cleaner floor. Always wear protective gloves and goggles when using a steam stripper, and follow the manufacturer's instructions for use.

2 Once the floor has dried, apply a coat of non-slip, silicone-based wax to the entire floor. Apply the wax with a cotton cloth, working it well into all areas.

3 Allow the wax to dry then buff up the surface to give a highly polished finish. An electric buffer is ideal, but a broom with a cloth pad attached works just as well.

6

# RENOVATING FLAGSTONES

F lagstones are generally the most heavy-duty form of hard tile floor, and they, too, require occasional maintenance. Periodic application of sealant and other minor repairs will keep flagstones in excellent condition and looking good for many years.

1 Joint failure within the flagstone can cause areas to flake away from its surface. Where these become deeper holes, use a hammer and cold chisel to remove the loose chips of stone. Wear gloves and goggles to protect your eyes and hands from any flying debris.

2 Dust out the area and dampen with a little water. Mix up some exterior filler or sand and cement. Adjust the amount of filler/cement added to the mix to achieve a reasonable colour match with the surrounding stone. Press it firmly into the hole.

3 Clean the remainder of the flagstones thoroughly then apply a proprietary sealant to cover the repaired area as well as the rest of the stone.

## CAUTION

Where flagstones have been laid without a dampcourse membrane beneath them, they often allow the damp to rise through them to evaporate into the atmosphere. In this case, sealing the flagstones is not appropriate as the sealant itself will not adhere to the flagstone surface, and applying it will also upset this natural drying process.

6

# INDEX

All illustrations by Chris Forsey. All photographs by Tim Ridley except for the following pages:

l = left, r = right, c = centre, t = top, b = bottom

Page 5b Camera Press; 12t Elizabeth Whiting & Associates; 12b Elizabeth Whiting & Associates; 13tl Dennis Gilbert/View, 13tr Camera Press; 42t Robert Harding Picture Library, 42bl Peter Reid/Houses & Interiors; 51bl Elizabeth Whiting & Associates; 56tr Nick Huggins/Houses & Interiors; 56cl Charles E Lamb/Robert Harding Picture Library, 56bl Peter Aprahamian/Robert Harding Picture Library; 61b Elizabeth Whiting & Associates; 65b Elizabeth Whiting & Associates; 67br Andrew Wood/ The Interior Archive; 69c Lizzie Orme/Robert Harding Picture Library; 71bl Elizabeth Whiting & Associates; 74bl Graham Rae/Robert Harding Picture Library; 75bl Elizabeth Whiting & Associates; 76bl Verne/Houses & Interiors; 78cl Camera Press; 79t Trevor Mein/Arcaid; 79b Fritz von der Schulenberg/The Interior Archive; 96b Tim Beddow/The Interior Archive; 107b Camera Press.